NETWORKING AND
DATA COMMUNICATIONS

Victoria C. Marney-Petix

RESTON PUBLISHING COMPANY, INC.
A Prentice-Hall Company
Reston, Virginia

Library of Congress Cataloging in Publication Data

Marney-Petix, Vicki.
  Networking and data communications.

  1. Data transmission systems.   2. Computer
networks.   I. Title.
TK5105.M355 1986   384   85-10886
ISBN 0-8359-4874-9

Editorial/production supervision and interior design
by Barbara J. Gardetto

© 1986 by
Reston Publishing Company, Inc.
A Prentice-Hall Company
Reston, Virginia 22090

10 9 8 7 6 5 4 3 2 1

PRINTED IN THE UNITED STATES OF AMERICA

NETWORKING AND
DATA COMMUNICATIONS

To Katherine Mayerhauser Schwarz
and to the memory of Leonhard Schwarz
for nurturing the best part of me

contents

Chapter 2
DATA TRANSMISSION   10

Chapter 3
INTERFACES   21

Chapter 4
PROTOCOLS AND ERROR
MANAGEMENT   34

Chapter 5
INTRODUCING NETWORKS   53

Chapter 6
LOCAL AREA NETWORKS   83

Chapter 7
PUBLIC PACKET NETWORKS   113

Chapter 8
VOICE, VIDEO, TEXT   127

Chapter 9
SECURITY 142

preface

This book is designed for business computer users, particularly the decision-makers who will consider local area networks and other communications-related technology during the 1980s, and the people who must advise these decision-makers.

Chapters 1 through 4 introduce you to data communications, Chapter 5 explains networks and their cousins, the multitasking and multiuser operating systems, and multiplexors. Chapter 6 treats local area networks in depth, while Chapters 7 and 8 cover public packet networks, voice technology, and teletext and videotex. Chapter 9 discusses security issues.

After the introductory chapters, each chapter includes checklists to help you determine what technology and solutions are best for your business needs. When complete, these checklists will give you a roadmap for your decisions.

Each chapter treats its subjects in tutorial fashion, making even the most technically demanding chapters easy to read. You will learn all the technical vocabulary you need to discuss the technology issues with business associates or manufacturers' sales representatives. Consult the Glossary for an abbreviated definition of the most important technical terms.

Read each chapter through once and complete all the checklists, using the book as a business decision-making tool. Then keep the book on your desk as a reference.

Victoria Marney-Petix

acknowledgments

Many people generously gave their time and attention to technical reviews and requests for information. I gratefully acknowledge the special assistance of Larry Nicholas and Edward Cooper of Sytek; Abraham Mazliach of Ungermann-Bass; David Bess, Mike Szabados, Grant Smith, and others of Intel; David Kline of Texas Instruments; Michael Mooradian and Brian McKinsey of TYMNET; Phil Belanger and Chris Riggins of Corvus Systems; Michael Tassano of Altos Systems; Dr. Hassan AlKhatib of the University of Santa Clara; Joseph Austin of Solo Systems; and Kathleen Roy of Zilog. Corvus Systems made a generous loan of equipment. Alexis Seddun provided user reviews and Valerie Matsumoto of Stanford University provided invaluable research assistance. The line drawings were done by Michael Tassano and Thom Thomas.

James Marney-Petix listened, edited, cheerfully took on much more than his 50 percent of the home responsibilities, and developed a new appreciation for cats as companions while the book was being created. Finally, I wish to thank my beloved computer for behaving itself during the crunch times.

NETWORKING AND
DATA COMMUNICATIONS

introduction
to computer
communications

Computers take in and manipulate information, which is called data. In order to communicate with a computer, you and the machine must use a common language. This common language implies that the information you give the computer and expect to receive in return must be packaged in particular ways.

This chapter discusses the specific way that we must package instructions and information when communicating with a computer.

BITS, BYTES, AND CHARACTERS

The modern world economy uses the base 10 number system. The number 512 specifies 5 hundreds, 1 ten, and 2 ones. From right to left, the value of the positions increases as a multiple of ten. You start with the rightmost position equal to 10 to the zero power, which equals 1. The generally accepted theory states that humans chose the base 10 number system because we have a total of ten fingers for primitive counting. The base 10 number system, then, rests squarely on basic human anatomy.

Your computer uses the base 2 number system, which also rests squarely on anatomy—computer anatomy. The basic electrical constitution of your computer's hardware allows a current to be running or not, a circuit to be open or closed. The base 2 system is known as the *binary* system because there are only two elements: 1 and 0.

Each 1 or 0 is a binary digit, or *bit*. A *byte* is the smallest number of bits that a computer will manipulate as a unit. For most of the computers that a businessperson will encounter, a byte is 8 bits.

A *character* is a specific symbol that cannot be subdivided into anything smaller. The letters of the alphabet, the numbers 0 through 9, special symbols like #, $, @, and what your computer sees when you press the CONTROL or ESCAPE keys are all characters. Each of the characters your computer can potentially recognize has a specific numeric value.

The number of bits in a character is usually the same as the number of bits in a byte. It doesn't have to be, though. If your computer uses two bytes instead of one byte to store each character, the number of characters the computer can store will not equal the number of bytes it can store.

The binary number system uses some specific terminology when discussing its elements 1 and 0; this terminology is the subject of the next section.

On/Off, Low/High, True/False

Data communications and networking use all three schemes—on/off, low/high, true/false—at different times to describe the basic binary nature of electrical circuits.

On/off is the easiest to visualize. Current is on, or it's off.

Instead of saying that a signal is on, you can say that a signal's line is *high*. When a signal is off, the line is *low* (Figure 1-1). (High/low actually refers to the voltage. A voltage difference is what causes current to flow.)

The elements of the base 2 system, 1 and 0, can also be expressed as a *true/false* pair. The most common convention makes 0 equal to false and 1

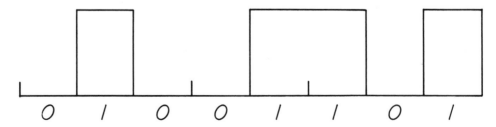

FIGURE 1-1
High or low, 1 or 0.

TABLE 1-1
Octal Constants

OCTAL VALUE	DECIMAL VALUE
177	127
205	133
357	239
25	21
BUT NOT:	BECAUSE
81	Octal has no 8
2F	Octal has no F

equal to true. This convention makes true greater than false because 1 is greater than 0.

In most cases, the terms true, high, and on are synonyms, as are false, low, and off. You will see all three systems used in this book.

OCTAL AND HEXADECIMAL

There are two popular number systems used with computers: octal and hexadecimal.

The *octal* number system, based on 8 elements, uses only the numbers 0 through 7 (See Table 1-1).

The other popular number system used with computers has 16 elements compared to the decimal system's 10. The *hexadecimal,* or *hex,* system uses the numbers 0 through 9 for the first ten elements, and the letters A through F for the decimal numbers 10 through 15 (see Table 1-2).

TABLE 1-2
Hexadecimal Constants and their Decimal Equivalents

HEX VALUE	DECIMAL VALUE
2FF	767
93D	2365
BUT NOT:	BECAUSE:
10,000	Hex has no comma
GDW	Hex allows no letters higher than F

Octal and hex give programmers a way to compress binary representations of numbers because 8 is 2 to the third power (cubed) and 16 is 2 to the fourth power.

CODES

Since computers deal only in numbers, you and your computer must agree on a set of numeric values for your set of characters. Computers represent characters internally according to a numbering convention called a *code*. The two most common codes are ASCII and EBCDIC.

ASCII

All commonly available microcomputers use the American Standard Code for Information Interchange (ASCII). It uses seven bits for character representation and includes an eighth bit for error detection. Since it is a 7-bit code, you can have up to 2^7, or 128, values.

You will frequently see ASCII referred to as a 7-bit code while ASCII uses an 8-bit byte. The two statements do not contradict each other. The

TABLE 1-3
ASCII Code (Decimal Values)*

Left digit(s)	Right digit 0	1	2	3	4	5	6	7	8	9
3				!	"	#	$	%	&	'
4	(	)	*	+	,	-	.	/	0	1
5	2	3	4	5	6	7	8	9	:	;
6	<	=	>	?	@	A	B	C	D	E
7	F	G	H	I	J	K	L	M	N	O
8	P	Q	R	S	T	U	V	W	X	Y
9	Z	[	1/8	]	^	—	`	a	b	c
10	d	e	f	g	h	i	j	k	l	m
11	n	o	p	q	r	s	t	u	v	w
12	x	y	z	{			}	~			

Codes 00 to 31 and 127 (decimal) represent special control characters that are not printable.

*From *Advanced Programming and Problem-Solving with Pascal* by G. Schneider and S. Bruell. John Wiley and Sons, Inc.: 1981, p. 499. Reprinted with permission.

TABLE 1-4
ASCII Code (Binary Values)*

High-order bits

Low-order bits

Bits												
				7	0	0	0	0	1	1	1	1
				6	0	0	1	1	0	0	1	1
4	3	2	1	5	0	1	0	1	0	1	0	1
0	0	0	0		NUL	DLE	SP	0	@	P	\	p
0	0	0	1		SOH	DC1	!	1	A	Q	a	q
0	0	1	0		STX	DC2	"	2	B	R	b	r
0	0	1	1		ETX	DC3	#	3	C	S	c	s
0	1	0	0		EOT	DC4	$	4	D	T	d	t
0	1	0	1		ENQ	NAK	%	5	E	U	e	u
0	1	1	0		ACK	SYN	&	6	F	V	f	v
0	1	1	1		BEL	ETB	'	7	G	W	g	w
1	0	0	0		BS	CAN	(	8	H	X	h	x
1	0	0	1		HT	EM	)	9	I	Y	i	y
1	0	1	0		LF	SUB	*	:	J	Z	j	z
1	0	1	1		VT	ESC	+	;	K	[	k	{
1	1	0	0		FF	FS	'	<	L	\	l	:
1	1	0	1		CR	GS	—	=	M	]	m	]
1	1	1	0		SO	RS	·	>	N	^	n	~
1	1	1	1		SI	US	/	?	0	—	o	DEL

*Adapted from *Data Communications: A User's Guide* by Kenneth Sherman. Reston Publishing Company, Inc.: 1981, p. 95. Reprinted with permission.

number of bits in the byte must include the error-detecting bit, but only 7 bits are needed to code the character value.

Table 1-3 lists the ASCII character values. First find the character you want a value for, then read the ASCII value, expressed in decimal notation (0 through 127).

You may also see the ASCII chart represented in binary notation. In Table 1-4, you find the character you're interested in and then read the

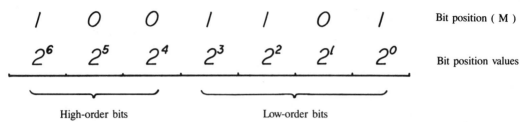

FIGURE 1-2
High- and low-order bits of the character M.

binary value from the row and column headings. The row headings give you the *low-order bits,* that is, the rightmost four bits in the 7-bit value. The column heading gives you the *high-order bits*. The rightmost bits are called low-order bits because they represent the smallest place values in the group of 7.

In Table 1-4, to find the ASCII binary value of the letter M, travel up the column and see that the low-order bits are 1101, then travel across the row and see that the high-order bits are 100. The ASCII value of M is 1001101, or 77 (Figure 1-2).

EBCDIC

IBM's large mainframes use Extended Binary Coded Decimal Interchange Code (EBCDIC). A character value has 8 bits, so EBCDIC defines 256 (2^8) characters, compared to 128 for ASCII. You may encounter EBCDIC code if your microcomputer sends or receives data from a large IBM mainframe or IBM network.

Although your ASCII system will not be able to communicate directly with an EBCDIC system (because the same bit pattern means two different characters in the two systems), ASCII/EBCDIC converters can translate one code into the other. The converter will be part of the sending or receiving system.

DEVICES

The history of the development of computer software shows a steady progression of removing programmers from the operational details of the systems they work with. Input/output to a printer was immeasurably more complex in the days when we had to position the printer head by sending a specific ASCII sequence, or insert the code for a carriage return and line feed whenever the printer needed to start printing on a new line.

Modern computers have drivers, compilers, operating systems, and other system software that shield computer users from the idiosyncrasies of the hardware. This frees computer users to deal with concepts rather than details and leads to greater efficiency because you can express your ideas in a nearly natural language.

In the early days of computing, there was only one kind of device in a computer system—the physical device. A printer, a modem, and a floppy disk drive are all physical devices.

Now we also have logical devices.

Logical Devices

The same technological evolutionary process that led to efficient operating systems and other system software led to the concept of the logical device. A *logical device* is a piece of software, a collection of data, or any other entity that you can send to, receive from, or otherwise manipulate. A disk file, the volumes that your Winchester disk is divided into, a floppy disk drive's controller, a printer controller, a modem's input buffer: these are all logical devices.

Some logical devices, like the floppy disk, are coexistent with a physical device, while others, like files on the disk, are not (Figure 1-3).

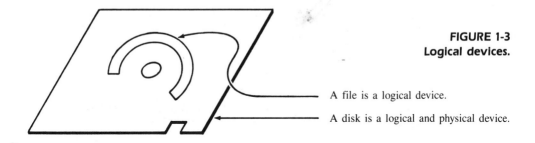

FIGURE 1-3
Logical devices.

A file is a logical device.

A disk is a logical and physical device.

One logical device can contain another logical device: a disk volume contains files, for example. These disk-related logical devices—your files, volumes, and disks—simplify computing tremendously. If you want to read a file, you simply tell your computer that you want to read the file named "Mktg.March83," in the current volume, on the current disk.

You *don't* have to tell your computer that you want the data contained in sectors 1–3, track numbers 2–4, etc. You deal strictly on the conceptual level with printers, plotters, disks, volumes, and other devices, which store, print, and manipulate their data without your detailed instructions on exactly how they should do their jobs.

Components of a Computer System

A computer system is usually composed of a keyboard, display, computer, and peripherals such as disk drives, printers, and modems. The computer's "brain," as well as memory, modems, and specialized software, usually exist on plug-in cards. The computer's brain is its central processing unit *(CPU)*.

Terminals.   A keyboard plus a display form an entity usually called a *terminal*. The word terminal comes from the Latin *terminus:* an endpoint. When we speak of two terminals, it doesn't imply that the terminals cannot actually be full-fledged stand-alone computers. It simply means that they are endpoints for a particular transaction. If one of the endpoints is controlling the transaction, we call that computer a *host computer*.

Terminals come in three types: dumb, smart, and intelligent. The dumb terminal is not a stand-alone computer and can do nothing on its own. All it gives you is an inexpensive way to connect to another computer. If you buy a mainframe computer's time through a service bureau, you are probably using dumb terminals.

Smart terminals can do a certain amount of local processing but need to be connected to a computer in order to accomplish any substantive task, like querying a database. Their major value is that they do not tie up a large number-crunching computer with low-level computing tasks. This is very important if you are buying time on the large computer, or if the computer is heavily loaded and must be used as efficiently as possible.

An intelligent terminal is a stand-alone desktop computer. The phrase "intelligent terminal" was coined to remind small computer owners that their machines can always be terminals to another, larger computer. For example, you could collect and massage a database and then transmit it to your company's national headquarters. The headquarters mainframe will see your computer as a terminal in its computer system.

Memory Devices.   Most computer systems use disks to store information. Floppy disks come in various sizes, with 5¼- and 8-inch disks most common. Their advantages are low cost and transportability. You can buy single-sided or double-sided, and single-density or double-density disks. Your system's disk drive will usually accept only one combination of side and density, although some systems can take a variety of disks.

You can also buy a Winchester sealed hard disk for your system. (Winchester means a sealed disk in the same way we refer to "floppy" disks—it is not a brand name.) Instead of the usual quarter-megabyte maximum of an 8-inch floppy disk, a Winchester disk drive can hold 80 or more megabytes. The sealed disk system also gives you lower error rates.

Winchester disk drives cost more than floppy disk drives and are much less transportable.

Other Components.   Printers and modems are the remaining common system items. A printer prints what it receives from your computer, and a modem lets you transmit information over a telephone line. Modems are discussed in detail in Chapter 2.

2

data
transmission

You're sitting in your office, generating spreadsheets, composing memos, and drafting correspondence with your microcomputer and printer. You're entirely self-sufficient for these tasks. But suppose that you want to communicate with the outside world: transfer a file of financial data to your home computer so you can look at it during the weekend, or transfer the next chapter of your Great American Novel from your home computer to your publisher, literary agent, or adoring parent? You need a modem.

MODEMS

In the days when there were no microcomputers, only monstrous mainframes doing payrolls, military ballistics calculations, and banking applications, computer designers first considered the problem of connecting computers to each other, across the country or around the world. The limiting factor was the length of the wire. In order to connect your computer to other computers you need a physical connection—a wire—between them.

The cost of stringing millions of miles of wires around the world was prohibitively high, as you might imagine, so the designers looked for another alternative. The answer they came up with is sitting on your desk: the telephone.

The telephone companies of the world have already strung wires connecting your office with every other office in the world. If computers could communicate with other computers over an already existing network of wires, computer owners would need to make no investment of their own. The solution was to modify the computer information so that telephone lines could carry it.

Your microcomputer uses *digital* data: the 1 and 0, ON and OFF method of coding information. Another way to code information is as a continuously graded, and then modulated, series of sounds. Sound and other media with continuously graded rather than binary values are *analog* media, and the sounds that the telephone system sends from one location to another are analog signals.

Digital data are turned into analog data as they pass through a *modem*. Another modem at the other end translates the analog sounds into digital data again. The word modem comes from MOdulator/DEModulator, and that's exactly what the modem does (Figure 2-1).

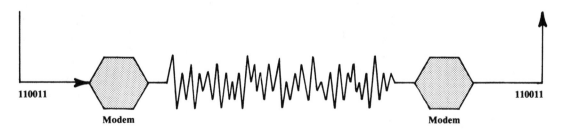

110011   Modem   Modem   110011

Digital Data   Analog Data   Digital Data

FIGURE 2-1
Modulation and demodulation.

Types of Modems

Modems come in two types: acoustic coupler modems and direct connect modems. The acoustic coupler has a cradle that you fit your phone into; a direct connect modem connects directly into a telephone wall socket or the back of the telephone.

If you have a portable computer, the modem that you can buy for it will almost inevitably be an acoustic coupler because acoustic couplers can use regular unpluggable telephones in hotel rooms and on street corners. An acoustic coupler is somewhat more error prone than direct connect, however.

Types of Telephone Lines

You have two more options after you've chosen a modem. First, what type of telephone line do you want?

The type of telephone line you will find in a residence, motel room, and most offices is called a *switched telephone line*. You pay regular telephone connect charges when you use a dialup, switched line. Transmitting data to Cincinnati for ten minutes costs the same as any other ten-minute conversation with Cincinnati.

You can also pay extra and get a *conditioned,* or *leased line* with a lower error rate. The telephone company's regular switched lines provide customers with high enough quality for normal conversation. Your data transmissions need a higher quality line—or you have to depend on your error-detection software to screen out the errors. Leased lines also support higher data transfer rates than switched telephone lines.

If you transmit data between a small number of fixed locations, a leased line is probably cost effective. If you must collect or transmit data from a large number of locations, you will have to make a choice between the expense of leased lines and the expense of error-detecting and correcting software for the switched line's higher rate of errors. Chapter 4's discussion of error detection and correction includes a checklist to help you choose.

ONE DIRECTION OR TWO?

Some modems can only transmit or receive, while others can do both. When you choose from simplex, half-duplex, and full-duplex, you are deciding whether you want a modem with only one capability or with two.

Simplex

A *simplex* link carries information in one direction only, either transmitting or receiving (Figure 2-2). A simplex link is the appropriate choice when a terminal in a field office only needs to send information to the main office and never needs to receive any information, for example.

The advantages of simplex include inexpensive installation and simple software. However, since you cannot send information in two directions, potential applications are limited.

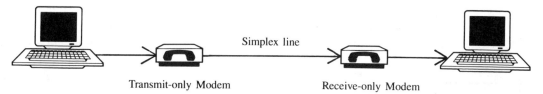

Transmit-only Modem   Receive-only Modem

FIGURE 2-2
Simplex data transmission.

Half-Duplex

For most applications, you need two-way (duplex) communication. The less expensive way of accomplishing this is with *half-duplex:* the line carries information in one direction at a time.

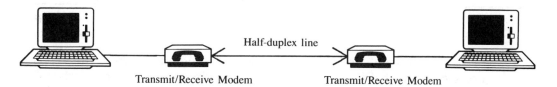

Transmit/Receive Modem   Transmit/Receive Modem

FIGURE 2-3
Half-duplex data transmission.

In a half-duplex system, the two endpoints or terminals of the line must communicate not only information but also their intentions (Figure 2-3). Suppose information is travelling from left to right; Terminal A is the sender and Terminal B the receiver. Terminal A finishes sending its data; Terminal B acknowledges receipt of the data and then requests the line.When Terminal A stops sending and begins receiving, you have *line turnaround* (Figure 2-4). When Terminal B finishes transmitting, Terminal A may request the line and it will turn around again.

You need more complex software to run a half-duplex system than a simplex or full-duplex system because of line turnaround. Also, the time the system must spend turning the line around is lost time. However, half-duplex gives you two-way communication at much less expense than a full-duplex system.

Full-Duplex

In a *full-duplex* system, information travels in both directions at once. This might seem to make full-duplex superior to half-duplex, but the situation is more complex than it seems.

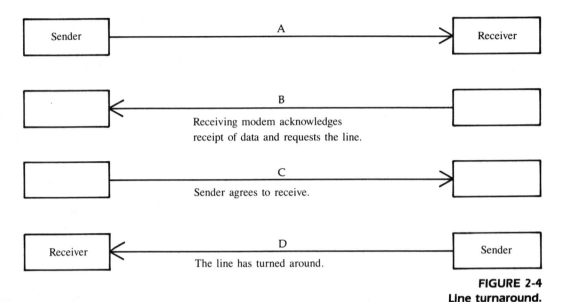

FIGURE 2-4
Line turnaround.

Since the data are transmitted as analog signals, you must also consider the *bandwidth*. When you transmit in one direction at a time, with simplex or half-duplex, you can use the entire *band,* or range of frequencies, the line has available. If you try to transmit in two directions at once, each direction can only use half the band. Therefore, a full-duplex system cannot rival the high speeds of a half-duplex system. (A leased line, if it uses four wires instead of the usual two, can give you high speeds at full-duplex.)

FIGURE 2-5
Full-duplex data transmission.

In a full-duplex system, each side can interrupt the other (Figure 2-5). Suppose your computer is receiving some routine updates from a field office when you realize that you need some information from the field that is much more important than the information they are sending you. Your commands to your computer regarding the information you need are passed on to the modem, which sends out an *interrupt.* This signal goes from your modem to the field's modem over your transmit band. The field's modem tells the field's

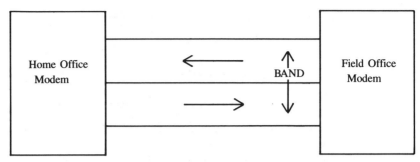

Each modem has a transmit half-band and a receive half-band.

**FIGURE 2-6
In full-duplex, each
modem can send and
receive simultaneously.**

computer that the home office has a high-priority request. They interrupt what they're doing to comply with your request.

With a full-duplex system, your modem can talk and listen at the same time (Figure 2-6). With a half-duplex system, your modem can only request to start sending when it has finished receiving. If it is sending, it cannot listen.

CHARACTER TRANSMISSION

Now that we've seen how modems work, let's move down to the level of the individual character of data. At this level, we are dealing with how the bits that make up a character move from place to place. The bits in a character use either *parallel* or *serial transmission.*

Parallel

With *parallel* transmission, an entire character is transmitted at a time: each bit has its own wire, and each bit is moving parallel to the other bits (Figure 2-7).

A particular wire will always carry the first, second, or fifth bit in the character. The bit positions of the wires do not vary.

You can only use parallel transmission over distances of less than 50 feet. Beyond this distance, radio frequency interference (RFI) becomes a problem, and the data signal itself becomes too weak. The components of your computer system (a printer, for example) frequently use a parallel connection; in general, the shorter the distance the faster the potential data transmission can be and the more attractive a parallel connection becomes vis-a-vis a serial connection (Figure 2-8).

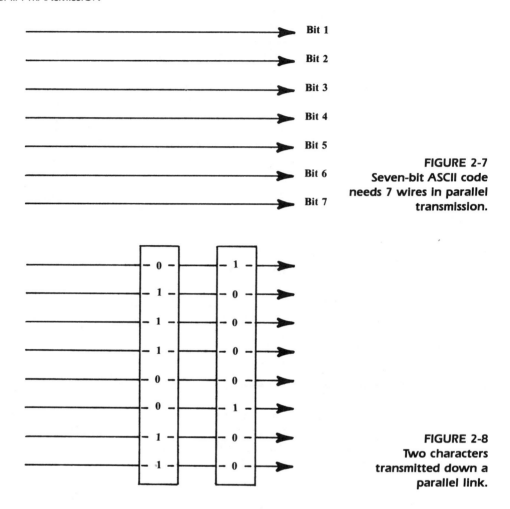

FIGURE 2-7
Seven-bit ASCII code
needs 7 wires in parallel
transmission.

FIGURE 2-8
Two characters
transmitted down a
parallel link.

Serial

With *serial* transmission, a character moves down one wire, a bit at a time. Figure 2-9 shows serial transmission of two characters. You can use serial transmission over long and short distances, making it overall the most common method of transmitting data. The rest of this chapter will deal with how serial data move from place to place.

FIGURE 2-9
Serial transmission of
two characters.

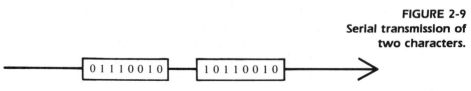

SYNCHRONIZATION

The first question to ask is: In serial transmission, how do you know when one character stops and the next starts? An even more fundamental question would be: How does the receiver know when to start looking for the first bit in the first character?

Both these questions involve *synchronization.*

Baud Rate

The receiver needs to know when to start looking for the first bit in the first character. After that, if the "clocks" at the two ends are running at the same speed, the sender and receiver will remain synchronized.

You can specify the speed of data transmission as a baud rate or as bits per second *(bps).* They are closely related, but they are *not* identical. The word baud comes from Baudot, an early method of encoding data. (The appendix includes more information on bps and baud.) As with apples and oranges, you can compare one baud rate with another, but you can't directly compare baud with bits per second. The most common bit rates are listed in Table 2-1.

You must set your two modems to the same data rate, and you must tell your computer what data rate the modem needs so it can transmit to the modem at the right rate. Unless there is a translator in the loop somewhere (one of the subjects of Chapter 5), all devices must use the same data rate (Figure 2-10).

TABLE 2-1
Most Common Bit Rates

LOW-SPEED TRANSMISSION
300
600
MEDIUM-SPEED TRANSMISSION
1200
2400
4800
HIGH-SPEED TRANSMISSION
9600
19200   (19.2 Kbps)

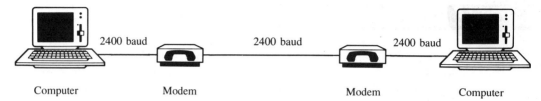

FIGURE 2-10
Every link in a communicating system must use the same (expressed in baud or bps) data rate.

Synchronization by Character

When you have set your data rate, your modem still needs to know when the bits it receives constitute a character of data. Serial systems have two choices: synchronous and asynchronous.

Synchronous Transmission.   In *synchronous* block transmission, the characters of data are bundled into *blocks* of standard lengths (frequently 256 characters) and the blocks, not the individual characters, are the transmission units (Figure 2-11). Each block is framed by start-of-text (STX) and end-of-text (ETX) characters.

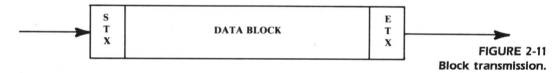

FIGURE 2-11
Block transmission.

During a transmitting session, the receiving modem will begin by seeing nothing but idle characters. Then the receiver will see two or more SYN characters. The SYN character gets the receiver synchronized, or "in sync." Now the receiver knows which bit is the first bit in the first character, and it can read the characters in the block that follows. After the SYN character, the receiver will see one STX character. Everything that follows, until the receiver sees ETX, is data (Figure 2-12).

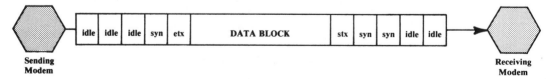

FIGURE 2-12
A typical block transmission sequence.

You will use synchronous transmission whenever you need high-volume, high-speed data transmission. Because data are packaged in blocks, your data transmission can be very efficient. You can buy synchronous communication software, sometimes sold as plug-in boards, for smart terminals and microcomputers.

You need not use block transmission to send synchronous data. As long as you use special characters (which vary from one standard scheme to another) to get the sender and receiver in sync, you can send unblocked bits. Bit synchronous transmission is still relatively uncommon in microcomputer applications.

Asynchronous Character Transmission

You cannot transmit interactive data—the character key you just pressed on your terminal, for example—in blocks. For this type of transmission, each character must stand alone. The receiving modem must synchronize itself to each individual character in asynchronous character transmission (Figure 2-13).

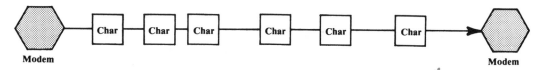

FIGURE 2-13
Asynchronous character transmission.

In *asynchronous* transmission, each individual character is framed by start bits and stop bits (Figure 2-14). The *start bit* tells the receiver that a character is coming, and the *stop bits* tell the receiver to wait for another start bit before sampling. The receiver knows how many bits should go into

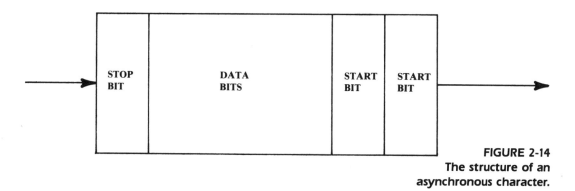

FIGURE 2-14
The structure of an
asynchronous character.

a character. It takes that number of bits and puts it into one character's space in storage. Most systems use one start bit and two stop bits.

FUTURE TRENDS IN DATA TRANSMISSION

Today's modems use the telephone network simply because it requires the least investment. Another, better solution may become common. Already, fiber optics, microwaves, lasers, and other technologies are under development.

3

interfaces

Interface, as a verb or a noun, has become the buzzword of the 1980s. People "interface" at noon instead of schmoozing over their lunches. But the English language is remarkably resilient, and if you have drowned in this misuse for some time, you probably have a good idea of what a computer's interface does.

An *interface* is a buffer zone between two devices or systems. If two devices don't speak the same "language," the interface must be a translator. If the data need repackaging, the interface obliges. For each device, the interface is a window to the rest of the world. In fact, most data communications problems lie not with the individual devices themselves but in the interface between them.

PORTS

Most devices are not plugged together directly; a cable of some sort connects them. The device has a *port* where it connects to a cable. As usual, a *port* is a physical as well as a logical device.

The device's physical port includes a plug that the cable's plug can seat into and special circuitry that handles data communication. Each device also has a non-static part of the interface—the logical port.

Since it is a software entity, you can alter the logical port at will. If the physical port contains more than one logical port, you can choose separate baud rates and other parameters for each logical port.

You will hear ports referred to as serial ports or parallel ports. You cannot switch a port from serial to parallel, or vice versa, through software. Serial and parallel interfaces require different plugs, as well as different circuitry, and work on different philosophies. In general, serial ports follow the RS-232-C interface standard and parallel ports follow the IEEE-488 interface standard. Both standards are described later in this chapter.

Device Drivers

Modern computers cannot sit idle—all their power wasted—while waiting for data communications. As you can imagine, data communications is a relatively slow process that progresses in irregular "bursts." Earlier computers had to interrupt other processing whenever data communications needed attention. This was too inefficient to continue.

Computer engineers developed hardware/software entities that deal directly with the data communications traffic on behalf of the CPU. These entities, called *device drivers,* deal with a specific device or class of devices. They collect incoming data until the quantity is large enough to be sent to the CPU for processing in an efficiently sized batch, and they act as an administrative/management layer between the CPU and the data communications traffic. Each device driver handles one or more ports (Figure 3-1).

At many points in a data communications system you will have powerful, extremely rapid computers coupled to relatively slow data communications channels. Efficiency requires us to find ways to keep the slow

FIGURE 3-1
A device driver controls ports that control devices.

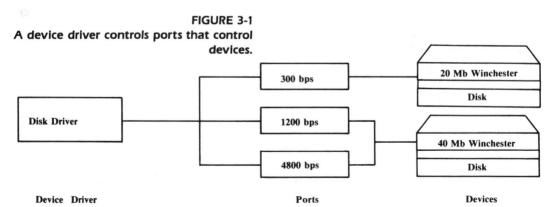

Device Driver	Ports	Devices

transmission channels from wasting the power and speed that the computers can give us. Chapters 4 and 5 contain additional solutions to this reoccuring problem.

STANDARDS

If one manufacturer made every computer device in the world, there would be no need for interface standards and there would be no interface problems. That is not and probably never will be the case, so computer manufacturers and users must develop standards, their essential common ground.

As in every compromise, computer-related compromises don't please everyone. However, these compromises, called *standards,* allow a buyer to put together a system composed of components from different manufacturers and communicate with other systems produced by different manufacturers. If you connect two devices that follow the same standard, you can be sure that the connection will not cause either device to burst into flames or suffer permanent electrical damage.

Several organizations develop standards in the United States. The American National Standards Institute (ANSI) is foremost among the standards promulgators. The ubiquitous "ANSI-standard" means that the item in question conforms to one of ANSI's published standards.

Alone or with ANSI, the Institute of Electrical and Electronics Engineers (IEEE) develops standards, including the 1983 IEEE-ANSI standard for the Pascal language. An association of professional electrical and electronics engineers, the IEEE includes a Computer Society whose members are active in the computer-related standards committees.

Another domestic organization that makes frequent contributions to the standards effort is the Electronics Industries Association (EIA), representing many electronics and computer manufacturers.

The international scene is dominated by the Comité Consultatif Internationale de Télégrafique et Téléfonique (CCITT) and its parent, the International Telecommunications Union (ITU), an agency of the United Nations. The International Standards Organization (ISO), a non-government body, works cooperatively with the CCITT. ANSI and the IEEE send representatives to the standards committees of the ISO and CCITT, which develop international computer-related standards.

The RS-232-C Standard

The EIA developed the RS-232-C serial interface standard because electrical compatibility is an essential first step in the communications process. (The CCITT has an international equivalent, called V.24.)

RS-232-C uses a 25-pin plug to ensure that:

1. The voltage and signal levels will be compatible.

2. The interface connectors can be plugged together because the pin numbers, configuration, and wiring will match.

3. Some control information matches.

Still, this doesn't seem like much, does it?

You're right, and it's an important point. RS-232-C compatibility is necessary but *not sufficient* if two devices are to communicate with each other. The fact that your computer and your printer both follow the RS-232-C (or any other) standard does not mean that you will be able to communicate anything over the interface. Unfortunately, there are a great many other things that must match if two devices are to send meaningful messages to each other, but electrical compatibility is an essential first step.

A Future Serial Interface

Actually, the RS-232-C standard already has a working successor. Developed by the EIA, RS-449 accepts higher data transfer rates and greater cable length, as well as more control lines. Over the next decade, it will slowly replace RS-232-C as the dominant serial standard. Most RS-449 equipment includes 449/232C adaptors that allow them to be used with RS-232-C devices during the transition period.

The IEEE-488 (GPIB) Standard

The IEEE established the IEEE-488 interface standard for parallel devices in 1975 and published a revised standard in 1978. ANSI approved the 1978 revised IEEE-488 standard, more popularly known as the General Purpose Interface Bus (GPIB).

A parallel interface connects a cluster of closely spaced devices, with no modem involved. Because GPIB operates with parallel devices, it creates a very different world from the RS-232-C world of serial devices.

A *bus* allows every device to access every other device. Each position on the bus has a number, called an *address,* or a *device number.* So device number 7 could send a message to device 5 or to devices 1 through 3. Because the bus-device interface is a logical device, you could remove a Winchester disk drive and replace it with another Winchester disk drive and the device number would not change.

The GPIB gives you eight data lines (since it is a parallel interface, all 8 bits in the ASCII byte travel in parallel, each on its own wire) and eight control and management lines. The data lines carry the data and the control

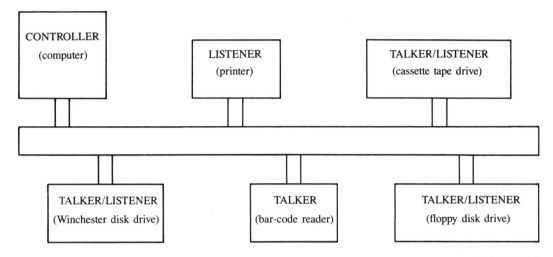

FIGURE 3-2
Six devices attached to the GPIB.

lines manage how the data are handled by the device that receives the data.

GPIB allows you up to 15 active physical devices (Figure 3-2), and these devices may be controllers, *talk-only* devices, *listen-only* devices, or devices that can both "talk" and "listen." Your microcomputer/controller can receive input from a talk-only sensor and send data to a listen-only printer.

In a typical parallel configuration, a bar-code reader (a "talker" in GPIB terminology) acts as a sensor. The bar-code reader talks to other devices on the bus, including a computer that identifies, prices, and totals the purchases and a printer that prints a receipt. Another common configuration uses a parallel interface to connect a computer to a printer. Chapter 2 discussed the advantages and disadvantages of parallel interfaces compared to serial interfaces.

DTE AND DCE

Before we discuss handshakes with serial and parallel devices, we need to introduce one more classification scheme—DTE and DCE.

A DTE (Data Terminal Equipment) device can be your computer, a printer, or another larger computer that you are communicating with. DCE originally meant Data Circuit-Terminating Equipment, and it still means that in the communications world, but you can remember it as Data Communications Equipment. A DCE is almost always a modem. In Chapter 5, we'll discover more examples of DCEs.

When you connect a DTE to a DCE, the DTE has the plug with the pins (what engineers call a male plug) and the DCE has the plug that the pins fit into (a female plug).

HANDSHAKING

Two spies meet in a crowded casino or on a murky waterfront and establish each other's bona fides through a dance of coded questions and responses. Similarly, when two devices are connected, they begin with an unvarying sequence of signals that serve as questions and answers. The two devices establish that each understands the other (or not) through this round of signals called a *handshake*.

The RS-232-C Handshake

A handshake prepares a communication channel that a particular sender and receiver can use. Whenever two devices need a new communications channel, this question-and-answer dance repeats.

Let's look at a typical handshake between two RS-232-C devices. Each side of the interaction has a DTE (a computer) and a DCE (a modem).

When a DTE and its DCE are first turned on, they must perform the first two steps of the handshake. The modem turns Data Set Ready on (or high) when it has completed all its self-checks and is ready to get to work. The DTE turns on Data Terminal Ready when it is ready to work (Figure 3-3). As long as these signal lines remain high, each device knows that the other is operational and ready to perform its functions properly. If one of these lines goes low, communications halt.

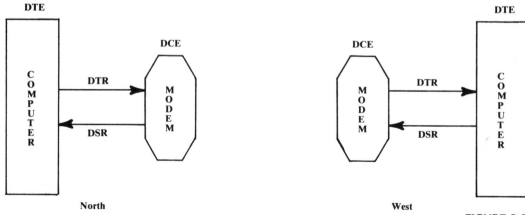

FIGURE 3-3
Data Set Ready (DSR) and Data Terminal Ready (DTR).

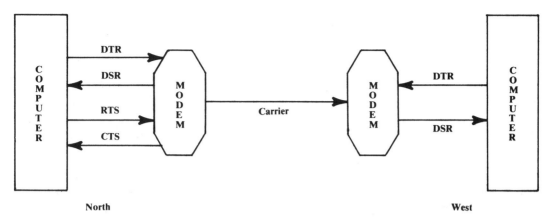

FIGURE 3-4
Request to Send (RTS) and Clear to Send (CTS).

The two computers North and West have completed the Data Terminal Ready and Data Set Ready phase of the handshake. Computer North wants to send some information to computer West. Since communication will occur from modem to modem, North must tell its modem what it wants to do.

Computer North turns on its Request To Send. If the modem is ready to receive and re-transmit data from North, it sends a carrier signal to West. The carrier signal, an unmodulated signal carrying no data, functions as an "I'm here." signal at this point.

After a built-in time delay to allow West's modem to detect the carrier and prepare to receive data, North's modem turns its Clear To Send on. Clear To Send tells North that the communications channel is clear and ready for data transmission. Notice that Data Set Ready, Data Terminal Ready, Clear To Send (CTS), and Request To Send (RTS) are signals involving only a DTE and its DCE (Figure 3-4). They are not communicated to West or its modem.

West's modem sees the carrier and lets its computer know by pulling Carrier Detect (CD) high (Figure 3-5). West and its modem prepare for the incoming traffic. The initial handshake complete, a communications channel is now ready for use.

When North has sent as much data as it intends to, it turns off Request To Send. North's modem responds by turning off Clear to Send and the carrier. When West's modem sees the carrier signal die, it turns off Carrier Detect. West sees Carrier Detect go low and knows that the line can now turn around.

If West wants to send, it turns on its Request to Send. West's modem sends a carrier signal to North and then responds to West with a Clear to Send. West is now ready to talk, as North is now ready to listen, and line turnaround—and this handshake—is complete (Figure 3-6). Table 3-1 lists the most important RS-232-C control lines.

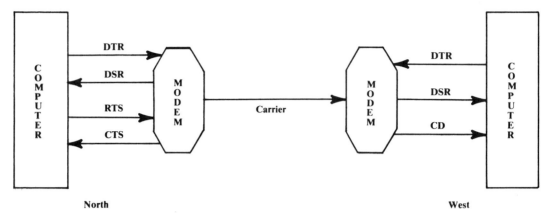

FIGURE 3-5
Carrier Detect (CD).

By the way, have you noticed that this is a half-duplex session? Devices will shake hands several times during a half-duplex session, whenever they have to establish a new communcations channel. Before the line can turn around, the two modems and their DTEs have to establish a new communications channel for the new sender and receiver.

The modems make the discovery that they do not have a communications channel in a roundabout way. Because the sending modem always begins to transmit data without verifying that the receiver is ready, the receiver cannot refuse to accept the communication before the sender sends. The receiver simply fails to acknowledge the data. When the sender does not get

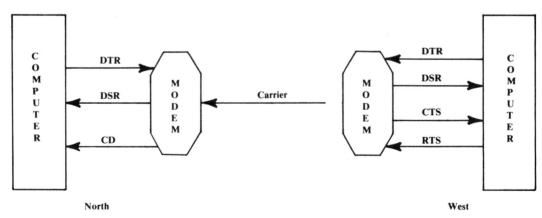

FIGURE 3-6
Line turnaround; West ready to send.

TABLE 3-1
Some RS-232-C Signals

SIGNAL NAME	MNEMONIC	PIN	PURPOSE
Request To Send	RTS	4	Terminal to modem
			Tells modem to prepare to receive and re-transmit data.
Clear To Send	CTS	5	Modem to terminal
			The modem's "yes" answer to RTS
Data Set Ready	DSR	6	Modem to terminal
			The modem is ready
Data Terminal Ready	DTR	20	Terminal to modem
			The terminal is ready
Carrier Detect	CD	8	Modem to terminal
			The modem detects a carrier from another modem (Another modem wants to send)

a data acknowledgment, it knows that no communications channel exists, if not the reason. Data acknowledgments are the subject of the next section.

Data Acknowledgment

If your system is full-duplex, the receiver has a transmit line and a receive line. The receiver uses its transmit line to *acknowledge* the data that comes in on the receive line. With a half-duplex system, you have to turn the line around before you can acknowledge the data received. Because turning the line around is a relatively slow process compared to data transmission, avoiding line turnaround is a plus. You don't want to go through a full-fledged handshake, turning the receiver into a transmitter just so the new transmitter can say "OK. Data received. Send some more."

Some half-duplex modems (with four wires) have a much slower secondary channel that carries nothing but these acknowledgment messages. Another popular solution is to precede each transmission with an acknowledgment of the last transmission received (Table 3-2). We will return to this subject in Chapter 4.

Data acknowledgment frequently uses the ACK character. (Go back to Chapter 1 and find the ACK symbol in the ASCII code chart, Table 1-4.)

TABLE 3-2
Data Acknowledgment

Solution 1	Full-duplex	User sends ACK on the transmit channel while data arrive on the receive channel. Or user intersperses ACKs of data received with other data on transmit channel.
Solution 2	Half-duplex	Slow secondary channel just for ACK messages. If the receiver sends a NAK, the sender must retransmit everything it sent since the last ACK.
Solution 3	Half-duplex	ACK the last data received. Then send new data. Together, the ACK and the new data form one message. Known as the "piggyback" solution.

The GPIB Handshake

When you think about the GPIB handshakes, you must constantly keep the bus structure in mind, with every device constantly connected to and monitoring the bus. The parallel connection is fundamentally different from the cable-connecting-two-devices serial world.

The bus can have only one *controller*—almost always a computer. The devices GPIB calls *talkers* put data on the bus, and the *listeners* take data off the bus. The controller can also talk or listen, depending on the type of controller it is. Figure 3-2 shows six devices attached to the GPIB, including

FIGURE 3-7
The controller (computer)
requests Device 2, but
Device 2 keeps the Not
Ready for Data control
line true.

"Device 2, are you ready?"   "Not Ready For Data."

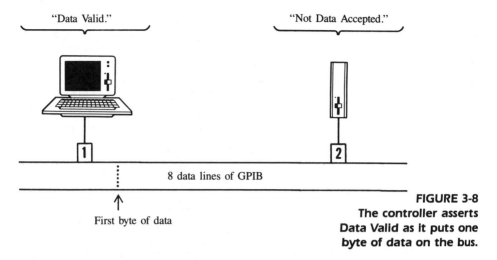

"Data Valid."

"Not Data Accepted."

8 data lines of GPIB

↑
First byte of data

FIGURE 3-8
The controller asserts
Data Valid as it puts one
byte of data on the bus.

talkers, listeners, and a controller. The eight control and management lines comment on the data that travel on the eight data lines.

A controller/talker (your computer) begins by putting the address of the device(s) it wants to talk to on the bus. All the devices listen for their address to be mentioned. If a listener sees its address, but isn't ready to listen, it leaves the control line Not Ready For Data (NRFD) true (Figure 3-7).

If the requested listener makes NRFD false, it is telling the computer that it is ready. The computer sees NRFD false and knows that it can talk. The talker asserts Data Valid (DAV) while sending data on the eight data lines (Figure 3-8). DAV means that a data byte is travelling down the data lines. (It implies nothing about error-checking.)

FIGURE 3-9
Device 2 makes Not
Data Accepted
momentarily false to
accept a byte of data.

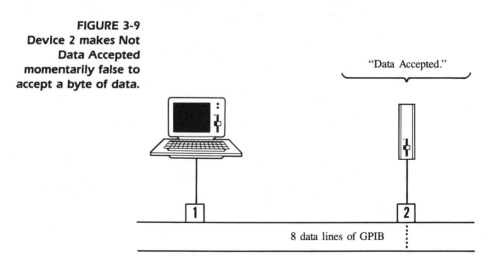

"Data Accepted."

8 data lines of GPIB

TABLE 3-3
Some Important GPIB Control Lines

SIGNAL NAME	MNEMONIC	PURPOSE
Attention	ATN	The controller makes this line true to request the attention of other devices on the bus, to prepare them for a handshake.
Data Valid	DAV	The talker makes this line true to tell the listener that a data byte is on the data lines.
End or Identify	EOI	Used at two different times. As END, it tells the listener that the current byte is the last byte; talking has ended. As IDENTIFY, the talker makes this line and the ATN line true, to ask "Who's out there?" This is the GPIB's poll. Chapter 5 discusses polls.
Not Data Accepted	NDAC	The listener keeps this line true while it takes the data byte from the bus and makes it false to accept the data byte.
Not Ready For Data	NRFD	The listener makes this line false when it is ready to receive data.

The listener leaves Not Data Accepted (NDAC) true until it has finished taking the data byte from the bus. It makes NDAC false momentarily to accept the data byte (Figure 3-9).

As long as the listener keeps NRFD false and the talker has something to say, data will flow down the data lines and will be accepted and acknowledged, byte by byte.

When the talker puts its last data byte on the data lines, it makes the End Or Identify (EOI) control line true. EOI means that the controller/talker has finished talking. The controller/talker can then request another listener.

Does this seem more complex than the RS-232-C handshake? With all signals phrased as negatives, the signals must be false in order to give a positive result. The GPIB signals seem more complex than they actually are because of these double negatives. Table 3-3 lists some important GPIB control lines.

BEYOND THE INTERFACE

Standard interfaces make it possible for devices to achieve basic electrical compatibility. A handshake creates a data channel so the two devices can communicate with each other.

But how do the two devices package their data so they both know what constitutes data? How do they recognize errors in the data they receive? These are the subjects of the next chapter.

4

protocols
and error
management

The Prime Minister steps from the plane and the strains of "God Save the Queen" waft over the airport's waiting throng. Then she is whisked away by limousine to the White House to meet the President and Vice President of the United States.

Diplomatic protocol requires the band at the airport, the limousine, and the personal meeting with the host country's chief executive.

Computer protocols have some elements in common with diplomatic protocols: you ignore then at your peril; greeting ceremonies must precede substantive discussions; the two parties must be of the same rank.

PROTOCOLS

A *protocol* is a strict procedure for establishing and maintaining communication between two objects in a communications system. Does that sound almost like the definition of an interface? A full explanation must wait for Chapter 5, but consider this: a protocol is a strict procedure for communications between objects of equal rank in a communications hierarchy while an interface is a translator between unequal and dissimilar objects.

Because a protocol requires two parties at the same level in the communications hierarchy, each level in a communications system must have its own protocol. The protocols of the data link layer in a communications system are called data link protocols.

DATA LINK PROTOCOLS

The *data link* layer in a communications system is the logical layer just above the physical layer that deals with signal levels, voltages, and other details of the physical medium. The data link layer deals with the data itself, how it is logically packaged to cross from one user to another. In order to understand the data link layer, you must have read Chapter 3.

Data link protocols come in two categories: bit-oriented protocols (BOP) and byte-controlled protocols (BCP). Byte-controlled protocols use specific control characters to inform the receiver when it is sending addresses or data and where the data bits start and end. The BCPs, in general, are older and more mainframe-oriented than the BOPs.

The bit-oriented protocol, instead of using specific control characters, depends on the position of bits within a field or block to signal its intentions. Since they use bit positions instead of specific control characters, the BOPs work the same with any code (ASCII or other).

Polling

Communication between machines or people frequently becomes intertwined with questions of power. *Polling* is one of these power-related issues.

When machines communicate with each other, they do so as equals or as unequals. When one computer controls how and when another computer interacts with the world, they are not equals, and this situation is part of the advantages or disadvantages that you must consider when buying this sort of power relationship. What are known as master/slave arrangements in large computer systems are called controller/subordinate pairs in microcomputer systems. Most protocols in common use today assume that one station in the communications system controls a number of subordinates.

In a controller/subordinate relationship, the subordinates cannot interrupt the controller. They must wait patiently until they are polled. When the controller sends ENQ (ENQuire) or a similar signal to a subordinate, it means "Do you have anything to send?" A subordinate cannot send anything anywhere, even to another subordinate, until the controller polls it, giving it permission to proceed. Each subordinate computer has an address, and the

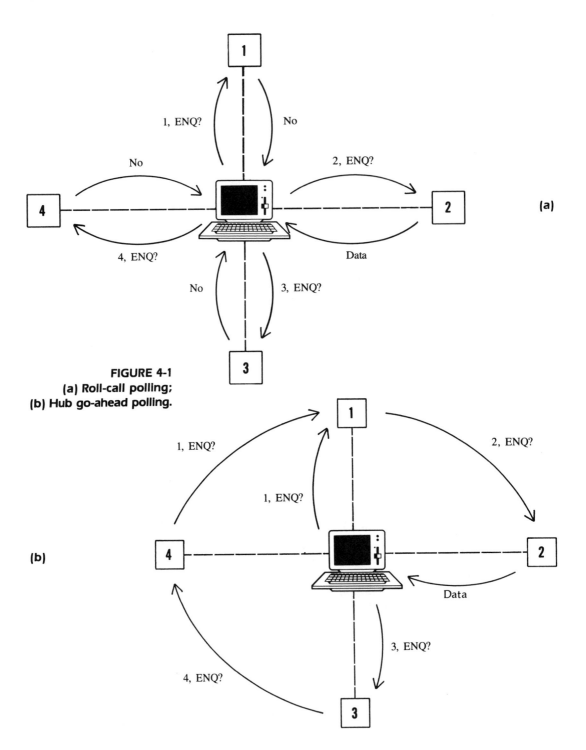

FIGURE 4-1
(a) Roll-call polling;
(b) Hub go-ahead polling.

36

address precedes the poll message. A subordinate ignores all messages that are not preceded by its address.

When one computer controls a number of subordinate stations, the poll frequently works in a roll call or *round-robin* fashion. The controller sends a poll to the first address and waits for a response. When the first address finishes sending, the controller polls the next address on the list. If the controller gets no response at all after a specific time period, it automatically polls the next address in the list. In this scheme, the controller spends a significant amount of time sending and receiving the polls.

You can also choose what's known as *hub go-ahead* polling (Figure 4-1). The poll begins when the controller polls the first subordinate address. If the first address has nothing to send, it does not respond directly to the controller. Instead, it passes the poll request to the next station. The second station can send data to the controller, leaving the controller to send a new poll to the third station when it finishes receiving the data. If the second station has nothing to send to the controller, it passes the poll on to the third station. Each station adjusts the address on the poll to the next station's address.

Hub go-ahead polling reduces the number of separate polls from the controller and therefore increases efficiency. However, the additional local processing at each subordinate address, in repackaging and passing on the poll, makes it more expensive.

Hub go-ahead polling also includes a danger not present in roll call systems. In a roll call system, if the controller gets no response to one of its polls within a specific time period, it automatically goes on to poll the next address in the system list. With hub go-ahead polling, if you don't remove a dead address from the list, the address that immediately precedes it in the list will attach the dead address to the poll. The system will come to a halt because a subordinate contains only enough intelligence to re-address a poll. The previous address in a poll list has no way of knowing that the dead address did not respond, and unfortunately neither does the controller.

You can give one address a higher priority than the others; perhaps it sits in the CEO's or Dean's office or its department interacts with the public and needs nearly instant response time. In this situation, the controlling computer will poll the higher priority address more frequently than it does the others. The response time can be adjusted as your business requires (Table 4-1).

If a modem is one of the addresses of your poll, the modem transmits the poll to another modem and ultimately to a terminal address.

When you use modems to poll addresses in different time zones, you can adjust the poll procedure so that the addresses only receive polls during business hours in their time zones (Figure 4-2). A computer in California should not be polling terminals in New York while it is polling terminals in Sydney. All three locations will not be active at the same time.

TABLE 4-1
Poll Priorities

AVERAGE WAIT FOR A CHARACTER AT THE TERMINAL WHEN A POLL ARRIVES	ADDRESS
2x	1
2x	2
x	3
5x	4
2x	5
5x	6

SO A SENSIBLE POLL LIST WOULD BE:

3
1
3
2
3
5
3
4
3
6

Polling becomes more time-consuming on a half-duplex line because the line must turn around with every poll. The controller transmits its enquiry, then the line turns around and the controller waits for a *yes* or *no* from the subordinate. When the subordinate finishes transmitting, the line turns around again and the controller sends out another poll. This gave system designers a strong motivation to reduce the number of separate polls in half-duplex systems.

Byte-Controlled Protocols (Bisync)

The most famous BCP, IBM's Binary Synchronous (Bisync) protocol, controls the transmission with special byte-length characters.

Bisync, also known as BSC, has several different control formats. Figure 4-3 shows two of the many BSC formats: one transmits data and the other transmits only header information.

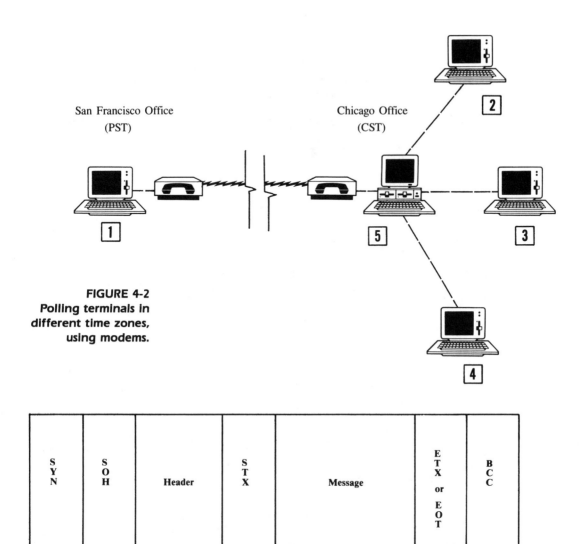

FIGURE 4-2
Polling terminals in different time zones, using modems.

S Y N	S O H	Header	S T X	Message	E T X or E O T	B C C

S Y N	S O H	Header	E T B	B C C

FIGURE 4-3
*Two Bisync structures:
Header alone and
Header plus message.*

SYN   SYNchronize. Establishes synchronization between sender and receiver.

SOH   Start Of Header. Tells the receiver that the text that follows, until STX, is the header.

Header   Identifies the receiver and contains other control information.

STX   Start of Text. Tells the receiver that the text that follows, until ETX or EOT, is the message.

Text   The message.

ETX   End of Text. Tells the receiver that the message is complete.

ETB   End of Transmission Block. See ETX. Used with Header Only formats.

EOT   End of Transmission. See ETX.

BCC   Block Check Character. Error-detection is discussed in detail later in this chapter.

After the SYN character synchronizes sender and receiver, the SOH (Start Of Header) character prepares the receiver for the Header that follows it. The STX (Start of Text) character tells the receiver that everything between it and the ETX (End of Text) character is text. EOT (End Of Transmission) signals the end of the transmission, not merely the text portion of a message. The last character, BCC (Block Check Character), contains error-detecting information.

The most striking difference between the BCPs and BOPs is in this use of specific characters to control the transmission and to separate the control information from the message.

Transparent Mode.   Because Bisync uses control characters to delimit the text message and header fields, you need special precautions before you can include control characters (like STX, SOH, and others) within these fields. If you send the ETX character as part of your message, the receiver will ignore the rest of the message. In normal mode, the receiver stops reading as soon as it sees the first ETX.

SYN	SOH	3	W	X	DLE	STX	T	H	E	STX	C	H	A	R	A	C	T	E	R	ETX	DLE	BCC	SYN	SYN

STX Character Inside The Text Message Field In Transparent Mode

FIGURE 4-4
Transparent mode.

Transparent mode temporarily disables this scanning process, allowing you to include control characters in the text (Figure 4-4). Simply bracket the STX and ETX control characters with DLE (Data Link Escape) characters. The DLE STX combination alerts the receiver to ignore all control characters it sees until the ETX DLE. The receiver will treat all characters as text while it is in transparent mode.

Control and Message Modes.   IBM's Bisync can only be used with a half-duplex operation, while some ASCII-standard byte-controlled protocols can use both half- and full-duplex. Because of IBM Bisync's half-duplex requirement, the subordinate has to answer ACK or NAK after the Header field and then again after the BCC. Each time the subordinate answers, the line has to turn around. All these line turnarounds lower the efficiency of the data link.

When the subordinate answers ACK to the Header, the controller knows that it can send the rest of the transmission; the receiver is ready to receive. This pause after the Header also changes the line mode.

Bisync has two possible line modes: *control mode* and *message mode.* When the two terminals are exchanging Header information, they are in control mode because the Header contains control information. When they are transferring the message, they are in message mode. The line turnaround after the Header field marks the shift from control to message mode. Of course, the sender can transmit a second Header to follow the first Header. In this case, the sender remains in control mode.

Some control sequences mean different things depending on what mode you are in. If a transmission error causes the receiver to go into a different mode than the sender was in, all the following messages will be misinterpreted. For example, SYN SYN NAK means "I am not ready to receive" in control mode, but in message mode it means "I am rejecting the last block of data I received. Please resend it."

Future of the Byte-Controlled Protocol.   Bisync and the other BCPs are still very popular, supported by a large installed base. You will probably encounter Bisync as you make use of external data bases and large mainframes.

Industry analysts agree that byte-controlled protocols are waning in popularity while bit-oriented protocols are becoming more common. An interesting BOP, also produced by IBM, is the Synchronous Data Link Control (SDLC) protocol.

Bit-Oriented Protocols (SDLC)

SDLC packages information into *frames*. Each frame divides into *fields,* each with a specific function:

- **Flag Field** tells the receiver that a SDLC-format field follows it.
- **Address Field** names the address of the secondary station.
- **Control Field** identifies the frame as a command or response frame, contains a poll bit and contains other control bit positions.
- **Information Field** can be any length, and follow any code (ASCII or EBCDIC).
- **Frame Check Field** contains error checking.
- **Flag Field** ends the SDLC frame.

All fields are eight bits long, except the Information Field.

Flag Field	Address Field	Control Field	Information Field	Frame Check Field	Flag Field

FIGURE 4-5
An SDLC frame.

Since all frames have the same structure, SDLC is simpler and therefore more flexible than Bisync. The Information Field, containing the data, can be any length of 8-bit bytes and can contain acknowledgments of previous messages as part of its content. In SDLC, each frame has a meaning that does not change. The protocol does not have modes that change the meaning of a character as Bisync does.

One station in the data communications link, called the primary station, takes responsibility for scheduling, starting, and stopping the communica-

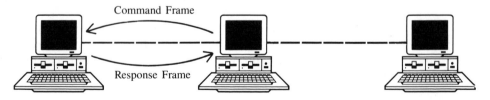

FIGURE 4-6
The primary station sends command frames while secondary stations send response frames.

TABLE 4-2
BSC or SDLC

Do you:	(check)
Need both full and half-duplex capability?	☐
Want error-checking on all frames or fields, not just the header and text?	☐
Want addressing in every frame?	☐
Want polling in every frame?	☐
Want to combine ACKs with data?	☐
Want the protocol to work the same, regardless of the network's structure?	☐
Want all or most transmissions in transparent mode?	☐

Count the number of checks. If you have more than two, seriously consider SDLC rather than Bisync.

tion. All frames sent by this primary station are command frames. The secondary stations send response frames (Figure 4-6). The secondary stations know who is supposed to receive a particular command frame by reading the address field. Stations 1–5 ignore command frames addressed to station 6.

Secondary stations cannot send to each other. All communication must be to or from the primary station, and the only address in the Address Field is the secondary's address. There is an advantage over BSC in that the primary can send a series of frames to different secondaries by varying the address field of the various frames. The line need not turn around when the primary station wants to switch from sending to station 1 to sending to station 5. The primary sends to all the stations it has messages for by concatenating all outgoing messages. Then the line turns around and the primary accepts messages from the secondaries.

In SDLC polling, the secondary station can only answer (be in response mode and transmit to the primary) if the primary sends a frame to the secondary with 1 (or yes) in the poll bit position. If the line is half-duplex, the line will turn around so the secondary can answer. On a full-duplex line, the secondary will answer directly, on its transmit band.

The Flag Field is the byte 01111110, the only thing resembling a control byte in SDLC. Whenever more than five contiguous bits occur in the data, potentially confusing the receiver, the sender adds a zero after the fifth 1. When the receiver sees the extra zero, it strips it out and treats the byte as data. This process, called *zero insertion and deletion,* occurs automatically.

SDLC does error-checking on all frames. In fact, SDLC's error-checking includes every bit in the frame, control bits as well as data bits. This means that SDLC, and bit-oriented protocols in general, can achieve higher reliability and lower error rates than Bisync in particular and BCPs in general. This was one of the driving forces in bit-oriented protocol development. Table 4-2 compares Bisync with SDLC.

Choosing a Protocol

You may be forced to use a particular protocol in order to have access to a particular mainframe or other resource.

If you have an opportunity to choose between Bisync and SDLC, examine the checklist in Table 4-1. The confusion of Bisync's different formats and line modes compares unfavorably with the unvarying structure of SDLC's frames. Bisync's control by byte-length control characters means that if any one of several control characters appears within the text portion, you must add an escape character to alert the receiver. SDLC only has one troublesome byte—the Flag Field that brackets the frame. If this particular bit pattern occurs in the data, zero insertion prevents any misunderstandings. SDLC's error-checking covers every field in the frame—another plus for the bit-oriented protocol.

Finally, although Bisync and SDLC are good representatives of the two approaches, they do not define the BCPs and BOPs. Use the general information in this chapter to make your evaluation of a specific protocol.

PRINTER I/O PROTOCOLS

One type of protocol is particularly relevant to your business life. The protocols of the computer/printer interface may actually be the largest cause of frustration in the entire microcomputer owning experience.

Of the several printer protocols, ACK/NAK and XON/XOFF demonstrate the two main philosophies of control of input/output.

The first question we ask is: Who controls the interaction?

ACK/NAK

In the ACK/NAK protocol, the computer sends a batch (usually measured in blocks, although the size depends on the computer) of data. An ACK answer means "O.K. Send me more." NAK (Negative AcKnowledge) means "I am rejecting the last block of data I received. Please resend it."

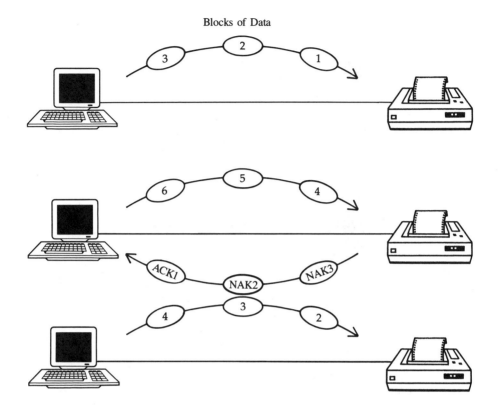

FIGURE 4-7
ACK/NAK protocol.

With ACK/NAK, who controls the interaction (Figure 4-7)? At first glance, the printer seems to, but look at the interaction more closely. The printer has a take-it-or-leave-it choice. It can't stop the computer in mid-batch and say "Stop, I'm not ready for any more right now. I'll let you know when I am." Perhaps the computer is sending data too quickly, threatening to overrun the printer's temporary storage area, called a print buffer. Perhaps the printer discovers an error in the last batch of data it received, or it develops a sudden electrical problem. Whatever the case, the printer must wait for the computer to finish what it is doing and then accept or reject on an all-or-nothing basis.

XON/XOFF

With XON/XOFF, the printer controls the interaction (Figure 4-8). The computer sends data as long as the printer keeps sending the XON character. XON means Transmit On, with X the old telecommunications

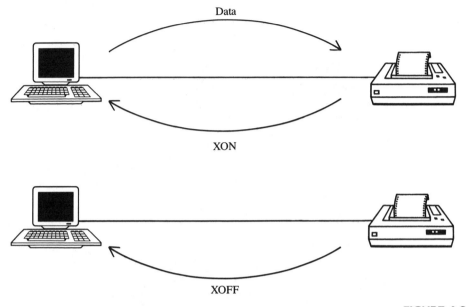

FIGURE 4-8
XON/XOFF protocol.

shorthand for "transmit." When the printer sends XOFF, the computer stops sending.

The DCl/DC3 characters do the same job as XON/XOFF. Look for them in the ASCII code chart, Table 1-4, which also shows ACK/NAK.

ERROR MANAGEMENT

No one likes errors. Nevertheless, we all know that total lack of errors is an impossible goal as long as we live in a business world populated by fallible human beings and their equally fallible creations.

In order to manage the tension between what you want and what you must settle for, you need to analyze errors and how they occur and then decide on a strategy based on the characteristics of your business.

Choosing an Error Management Strategy

Error reduction seems easy. You should discover the factors that lead to errors and then eliminate those factors. For example, some factors that encourage errors are: voice-grade (dialup) rather than conditioned lines; high load times, when your data communications traffic competes for the resources of an already heavily loaded voice system; larger block lengths. You could switch from dialup lines to conditioned lines, transmit over your dialup lines in the evening hours, or use smaller blocks of data in your transmissions. But it's not that simple. Leased lines cost more than dialup lines, employees prefer to work during the day and spend evenings with their families, and smaller blocks mean lowered efficiency with less information transferred in each minute of connect time. To make these and other more complex decisions, you need an error management strategy.

Deciding on an error management strategy is analogous to deciding on an insect pest management strategy. In the earlier view, the job of the farmer, agriculture official, or entomologist was to kill the bugs. All of them. This frequently required damage to the environment and to human health. The more contemporary strategy is to speak of managing the pest. You allow the pest to remain present in very small, controlled populations, exerting enough external pressure to keep the pest from significant damage while not exerting the kind of pressure that requires damaging the environment or its people. You accept a certain pest level in exchange for less damage to your ecosystem as a whole.

Preparing an error management strategy also requires you to make this kind of cost/benefit analysis. You need not pursue a zero errors policy for all applications under all conditions. You must decide, realistically, what level of errors your business can tolerate—bearing in mind the indirect but very real costs of consumer rage, if your error rate becomes too high—and how much you must spend to reach that error rate.

Sources of Data Communications Errors

In order to manage errors, you need to understand how and when they occur (Table 4-3).

Spikes, or *impulse noise,* cause the greatest number of errors in all types of data communication lines. What you would hear as a crackling noise in a voice communication can cause an entire group of bits to flip their states (from 1 to 0 or vice versa). Spikes occur because of voltage irregularities in the telephone switching equipment, lightning and other meteorological electricity during transmission, and faulty connections at various locations in the communications link.

The unavoidable thermal agitation of electrons generates what we colloquially refer to as hiss or static. This Gaussian, or white, noise does not cause significant problems. The appendix includes the equation for calculating the decibel, a measure of the offensive power of white noise.

Truly catastrophic data loss occurs with a line outage. This outage need not last long. Several seconds of outage destroys thousands of bit values. Lightning storms and faulty equipment cause this type of catastrophic loss.

TABLE 4-3
Sources of Data Communications Errors

	REDUCIBLE?	INCREASES WITH DISTANCE?	SIGNIFICANT SOURCE OF ERRORS?
Lightning and other meteorological phenomena	N	Y	Y
Faulty electrical circuits or dirty electrical connections	Y	Y	Y
Thermal activity of electrons	N	N	N
Impure carrier signal	N	N	N
Amplitude or frequency changes	Y	Y	N
Interference	Y	Y	N
Loss of power	Y	Y	N

With attenuation errors, you lose the high frequency component of the audio signal more quickly than the low frequencies, distorting the data that the receiver sees.

Amplitude errors come from a sudden drop in power caused by dirty electrical contacts, sudden changes in the electrical load, and switching errors.

Phase jitter, or lack of a pure carrier signal, is impossible to eradicate because no electrical equipment will ever be able to generate a pure carrier signal. It will always jitter or wobble to some extent, and this changes bit patterns.

Have you ever heard another conversation in the background during a telephone call? That *cross-talk* occurs on your data communication lines also, causing errors. Intermodulation noise, similar to cross-talk and usually created by a faulty modem, comes from interference between two signals. You can also see intermittent errors because of echoes on the data lines.

Finally, most of these errors do not alter isolated bits. Errors usually occur in bursts, called *burst errors,* and are the most difficult to detect and correct.

Table 4-3 shows that the major reducible source of data communication errors is impulse noise, which increases with distance travelled. Since faults on the switched telephone network cause most impulse noise, to reduce these errors you could use a conditioned line.

Strategy I: Accept Errors

The simplest strategy of all, you can accept whatever errors occur during transmission. This strategy is appropriate where errors are at worst mildly embarrassing. Text transmission might qualify for a laissez-faire attitude to errors if the text does not contain many numbers.

Strategy II: Detect and Retransmit

With this strategy, the receiver detects errors in a block and the sender retransmits the entire block. This type of error-handling software, not very complex to understand, use, or pay for, relies on an acknowledge/negative acknowledge scheme. It need not use the specific characters ACK and NAK in following this strategy. Figure 4-7 shows the ACK/NAK scheme in use as a printer protocol.

This approach has some disadvantages. The receiver must reject the entire block if it finds one error, and the entire block must travel over the lines for a second time. This reduces the efficiency of the transmission. It also may encourage you to use smaller blocks, increasing the overhead even more. The inherent unsophistication of this error-handling scheme means that it simply cannot detect the more complex burst errors.

Parity Checking.   Do you remember that ASCII code has seven data bits and a eight-bit byte? That "extra" bit is a *parity check* bit (Table 4-4). To calculate the parity bit, count the number of 1's in the seven data bits making up the byte. In an odd parity scheme, the total number of 1's in the eight bits must be an odd number. If you find an even number of 1's in the seven data bits, you must add another 1 in the eighth place to make the number of 1's odd.

TABLE 4-4
Parity

DATA BYTE	PARITY	RECEIVER ANSWERS
10001010	Odd	ACK
10001010	Even	NAK
10001101	Odd	NAK
00111111	Even	ACK
01011000	Even	NAK
01011000	Odd	ACK

Suppose you have 1010010 (an ASCII R) and parity is odd. You have three 1's and 3 is an odd number so you add a 0 to the eighth place to make the byte 01010010. As you send each byte, the receiver gets two kinds of information: seven data bits and a parity bit that tells the receiver whether or not the data bits have been tampered with en route. A receiver that sees 10010101 would have to answer with a NAK if parity is odd. The receiver knows that one of those data bits is an error.

Simple parity checking is vulnerable to combinations of errors. It can detect one error, but what about two? If two bits flip their values, the parity bit will not alert the receiver. Any byte with an even number of errors will pass with errors undetected. This is cause for concern since most errors occur in bursts.

Redundancy Checking.   Longitudinal redundancy check (LRC) and vertical redundancy check (VRC) develop the basic parity idea on a much larger scale (Figure 4-9). Most schemes that use one, use both.

Consider the block of data shown in Figure 4-9, where the seven bits of an ASCII byte are arranged vertically. The eighth bit is the VRC bit. Longitudinally, the bit values contribute to LRC characters (which are 1-byte sized in this case). The bits in position 1 of each ASCII byte contribute to the first LRC calculation, the bits in position 2 contribute to the second LRC and so on.

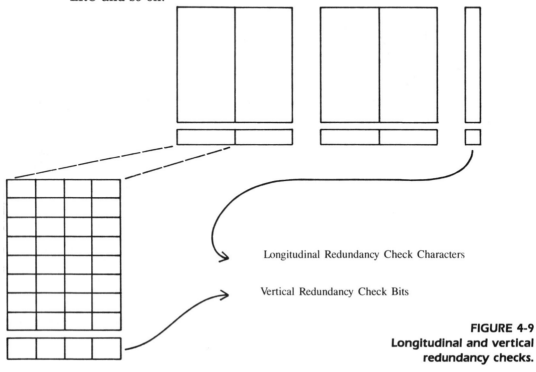

Longitudinal Redundancy Check Characters

Vertical Redundancy Check Bits

FIGURE 4-9
Longitudinal and vertical
redundancy checks.

Block of Data   CRC Character

FIGURE 4-10
Cyclical redundancy
check.

Using VRC and LRC together multiplies your chances of finding an error because each data bit contributes to two parity checks—the LRC character in its row and the VRC bit in its column.

The *cyclic redundancy check* (CRC) uses a check character at the end of a group (usually a block) of data (Figure 4-10). The sender calculates vertical and longitudinal parity according to a polynominal code and sends this parity character along with the data. The receiver calculates the proper parity character from the data and compares its calculation with the parity character that was sent. If the two characters are identical, the receiver acknowledges receiving the data.

CRC's other name, polynomial check, comes from the polynomial used in its calculation. The Block Check Character (BCC) in a Bisync block and the Frame Check Field in an SDLC frame are almost always a CRC.

Strategy III: Detect and Correct

Detect and correct, also known as forward error correction, works by calculating relationships between check bits and data bits. The maximum protection comes from schemes that include as many check bits as data bits.

This maximum protection would be appropriate for banks and other financial institutions where it is not acceptable to have high error rates in such data as customer account numbers, balances, transfers of funds, and so on. One mistransmitted digit can have disastrous results.

Because it must pinpoint errors exactly, and then reconstruct what the original data bits must have been, error-correcting software is much more complex than error-detecting software.

If you consider this error management strategy, you must be aware of the disadvantages. Premier among them is cost. Error-correcting software costs more than error-detecting software. Complex software must also inevitably introduce its own errors. Whenever you add a layer of software to any system, you add the possibility of errors and the errors increase with the complexity of the software. You must also consider the costs of repairs to your more complex solution. Finally, error-correcting software introduces more delays than error-detecting software, although only the most time-critical applications would notice the delays.

Hamming Codes

This error-correcting code type intersperses data and parity bits in a specific pattern. If one or more parity bits shows the wrong value (1 when it should be 0 or vice versa), there is an error. The error will then be tracked down by examining which parity bits failed. Since one data bit will affect more than one parity bit, your software can calculate which bit has flipped its value and will change it back to its correct value. When burst errors change many bit values, the software's calculations become very complex.

The Hamming code software in the receiver adds the parity bits to the data stream, and the software in the receiver uses the parity bits to correct any errors, stripping the parity bits from the data stream.

A CHECKLIST FOR ACTION

Now you are ready to construct an error management strategy, based on the relative costs of the error and the solution.

TABLE 4-5
Three Error-Management Strategies

	NO ERROR RECOVERY	DETECT AND RETRANSMIT	DETECT AND CORRECT
Type of transmission	Text	Critical text and numbers	
Potential damage factor	Low	Moderate	High
Retransmission necessary	N	Y	N
Cost of added software	N	Y	Higher
Errors introduced by software	N	N	Y
Time for Repairs	N	Y	Y
Copes with burst errors	Varies	Usually Y	Y
Software causes delays	N	Y	Higher

Table 4-5 summarizes the three main error management strategies. Notice that Solutions II and III introduce errors of their own, efficient as they are in rooting out transmission errors. Solutions II and III also work exclusively with blocks of data, requiring synchronous data.

The next chapter begins the study of networks, their predecessors, and alternatives.

5

introducing
networks

A spectrum exists from simple resource-sharing to large-scale private and public networks. This chapter explores the spectrum from resource-sharing to local area networks. Perhaps all you need is a multitasking operating system. Perhaps all you need is the pseudo-network that a multiplexor provides. And perhaps you need a true network.

The challenge is deceptively simple. How do you make the most effective use of scarce, expensive resources? There are many ways to accomplish this goal. Within this broader question, the place to start is: Do I need a network or would something else do the job that I need doing? (In this chapter, "network" means local area network.)

When you finish this chapter, you will be able to say to the multiplexor manufacturer's sales representative: "My solution must include the mux as a component of a full-fledged local area network because..." You can say to the local area network's sales representative: "I don't need a local area network, because..." In each case, what follows the "because" will be based on a well thought-out analysis of your business needs and the state of the technological art.

WHAT A NETWORK ISN'T

Although sometimes referred to as networks, all the technologies discussed in this section of the chapter fail to fit the definition of a network in one or more ways.

Resource-Sharing

Resource-sharing per se does not create a network. At the most primitive level, every operating system provides resource-sharing. The operating system arranges access to the peripherals and other system resources, and manages the amounts and kinds of access that specific users have.

The most common microcomputer operating systems, including CP/M and MS-DOS, are one-user, one-machine operating systems.

We judge an operating system by how efficiently it manages system resources, with the talents of an air traffic controller (in its scheduling activities) and a homemaker (in its frugal use of resources). By this criterion, multitasking and multiprogramming operating systems rate far above today's common microcomputer operating systems (Figure 5-1).

A multitasking operating system lets you run several tasks at once. For example, you could be calculating sums, processing words into paragraphs, and collecting data from a modem at the same time. Each one of these tasks, or jobs, can be active at the same time on your system.

The multiprogramming operating system serves many active users. (The terminology can be confusing. One person can generate many jobs, and each job is technically a user. So an active multi-user system could have only one human user.) With this arrangement, the operating system must prevent the jobs from interfering with each other. The CPU must give its attention to more than one job but can only do one thing at a time. The operating system's task in this type of system is to help the CPU pretend to do many things at once.

In general, the multiprogramming operating system does this in one of two ways:

1. It responds to one job until that job runs out of requests or until the CPU can delegate to another, slower process (like I/O). It then moves on to the next job.

2. The CPU gives one job its undivided attention for a specific period of time, then switches to the next job, which receives its undivided attention for the same period of time, and so on. The time period that the CPU devotes to each job is called a time-slice.

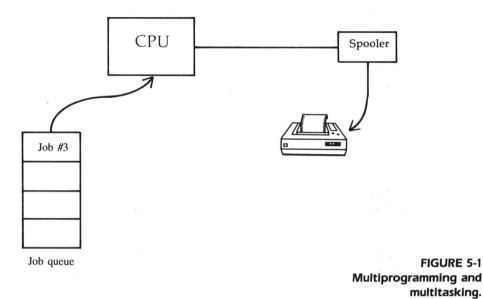

Job queue

FIGURE 5-1
**Multiprogramming and
multitasking.**

In both strategies, the operating system moves from job to job in a round-robin fashion.

Multiple jobs commonly share the I/O facilities through spooling. When the job needs I/O, the CPU passes the job (the file that needs to be printed, for example) to the spooler, which controls the spool operation. In most cases, jobs will print in the order they were sent to the spooler.

Operating systems designed for mainframes use other techniques to expand the memory capabilities of the system. With a virtual memory system, your job appears to have an infinite amount of memory available to it, as well as the undivided attention of the CPU.

In the future, the full computing power of today's mainframes—including multiprogramming, multitasking, and virtual memory systems—will be available in desktop computers. Regardless of how powerful and complex tomorrow's microcomputer operating systems become, they will still give you nothing more than an operating system's resource-sharing, the first step in a progression that leads to networks—local area and international, private and public.

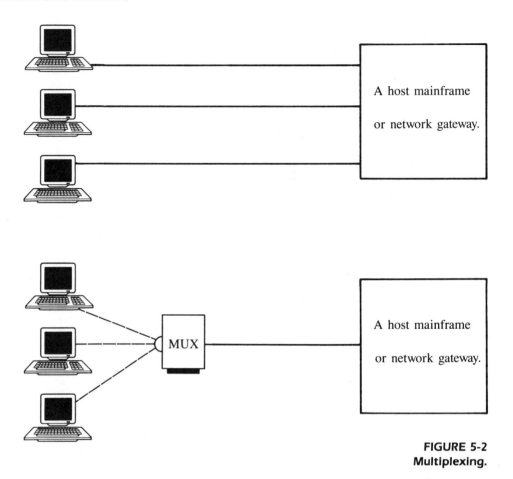

FIGURE 5-2
Multiplexing.

Multiplexing

The data communications interactions we've discussed so far are all point-to-point transmissions with one sender and one receiver. Multiplexing is one-to-many rather than one-to-one data transfer (Figure 5-2).

A *multiplexor*, or mux, acts as an agent for several (almost always video) terminals. The multiplexor collects the traffic for the terminals in some way and sends it to the computer over one wire rather than several.

Without a mux, every device would have to send data on its own low-speed line, wasting channel capacity and cluttering the office with wires. Multiplexing can give you considerable cost savings, regardless of whether it is several independent computers or several dumb terminals that you link to the communications channel. Dumb terminals and microcomputers are both low-speed transmitters while the communications channel is a high-speed line.

The challenge that the multiplexor has to face is how to take one communication channel with a finite bandwidth and divide it so that several terminals can use it, and so that the two ends of the communication—the terminals and the large computer—know which data belong to which terminal. The way that the multiplexor divides the scarce resource—the communication channel—determines the type of multiplexor it is.

Multipoint and Multidrop.   There are two ways that you can arrange to receive multiplexed data. If you have one receiver that demultiplexes the entire data stream and routes the data to the respective terminals, you have a multipoint system. If your data stream will go to a first destination, drop part of its data, then move on to a second and subsequent destinations, you have a multidrop line (Figure 5-3).

The crucial difference is that multipoint really only has one destination as far as the sender is concerned. The sender sees only the mux, not all the ultimate endpoints. Some techniques that you can use with a multipoint arrangement, you cannot use with multidrop because of the fundamental difference in the way it demultiplexes.

Frequency Division Multiplexing (FDM).   The frequency division multiplexor (FDM) takes the communication channel and divides it into *subchannels* of specific frequency range (Figure 5-4). Each subchannel belongs

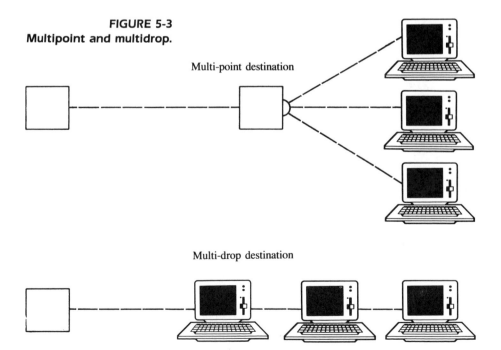

FIGURE 5-3
Multipoint and multidrop.

Multi-point destination

Multi-drop destination

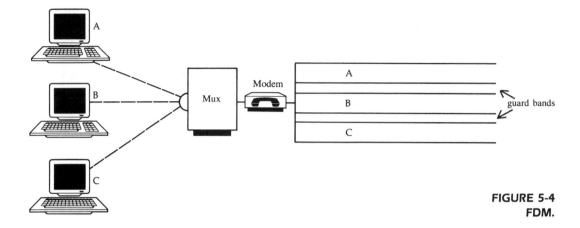

FIGURE 5-4
FDM.

to a particular terminal and is never used by another terminal. This means that you don't need your software to identify the data as coming from a particular terminal since all data on the subchannel belong to one and only one terminal.

Each subchannel must have *guard bands*—unused frequencies on either side of it—to prevent accidental leakage of data from one subchannel to another. This leakage, another form of the cross-talk discussed in Chapter 4, can be reduced but never eliminated. Particularly popular for short distances, most FDMs use RS-232-C connections to their terminals.

The U.S. telephone system uses frequency muxes to divide a voice-grade channel (the telephone cable) into separate subchannels for different conversations. Regular AM and FM radio stations also divide the available frequency range: each station uses a narrow band of frequencies for transmitting. The Federal Communications Commission allocates the available bands into subchannels for the different stations. The FCC makes an effort to keep the stations from interfering with each other, establishing guard bands of unused frequencies on the sides of each station's channel and regulating the power levels of the stations to limit their range. The stations must monitor their transmissions several times per day to ensure that the transmitter does not wander into the frequencies set aside for guard bands or into another station's channel.

Frequency division multiplexing has always been very popular because it is relatively easy to understand and implement. FDM also has the advantage of supporting both multidrop and multipoint lines.

FDM's major disadvantage comes from its major advantage—the dedicated nature of each subchannel. If a terminal is not sending or receiving, the frequencies lie unused. Unused frequencies on one subchannel cannot relieve congestion on another subchannel. FDM's allocations, inflexibly rooted in hardware, cannot be changed through software. You must pur-

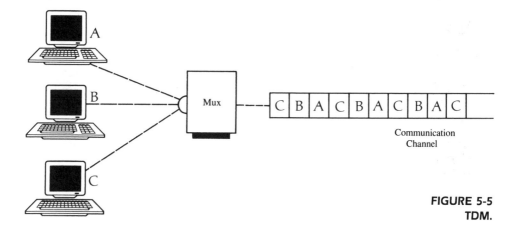

FIGURE 5-5
TDM.

chase an entirely new FDM if you want to change the number of channels in your system.

The next form of multiplexing requires more sophisticated software, but also has a higher efficiency.

Time Division Multiplexing (TDM).   The time division multiplexor (TDM) takes the communication channel and gives the entire bandwidth to each terminal for a specific period of time. The TDM cycles past each terminal in turn, accepting input during the terminal's assigned time slot (Figure 5-5).

A bit TDM takes the data from each terminal a bit at a time, while a byte TDM takes bytes at a time (Figure 5-6). Every process requires overhead, and the TDM is no exception. In this case, you must expect a separation between the time slots, constituting unusable dead time, known as guard bands just as with FDM. You must expect more overhead with a bit mux than with a byte mux.

Whether it is a bit mux or byte mux, each TDM assembles the data it collects from all the terminals into a frame and transmits the frame. (TDM uses the word "frame" just as the SDLC protocol did in Chapter 4. These are not identical to SDLC frames.) The receiving mux demultiplexes the frame and routes the data to the correct receiver, based on the data's position in the frame. The first character or bit will always be from the first terminal. The first, second, and other terminal positions are determined when you install the TDM and don't change. This scenario is called the fixed-frame approach. You can also have variable frames (Figure 5-7).

In a variable frame TDM, each frame carries data from only those terminals that actually have data to transmit. If terminals 1 and 3 have data for the frame, but terminals 2 and 4 do not, the variable frame approach means that the frame will contain the data from terminals 1 and 3 but will

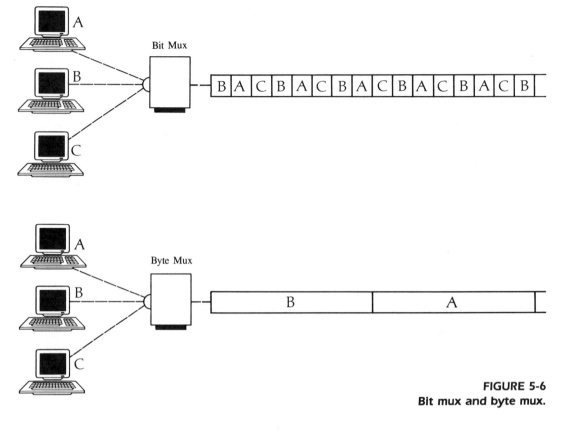

FIGURE 5-6
Bit mux and byte mux.

not reserve space in the frame for terminals 2 and 4. In this case, the frame includes control information to tell the demultiplexing TDM which terminals have included information in the frame. For the small increase in overhead caused by the control information, you avoid the wasted time slots for terminals that are not sending.

Isochronous (from Greek word stems meaning "same time") time division multiplexing gives you the opportunity for more freedom with your terminals. In general, a mux has a master clock and forces the terminals to provide data in accordance with timing signals from this master clock. The isochronous TDM collects data that the terminals send according to their own internal clocks. The mux collects the data into buffers and then transmits it according to its master clock. But it does not impose its own timing on the terminals. You will find this an advantage if your terminals differ widely in their internal timing because the mux can handle them all without requiring them to change their internal operations.

The TDM gives each terminal the entire bandwidth for a specific, albeit short, time period. Therefore, you can expect a TDM to be more efficient

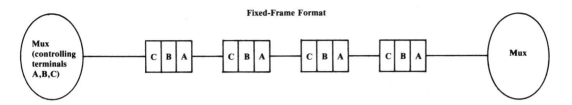

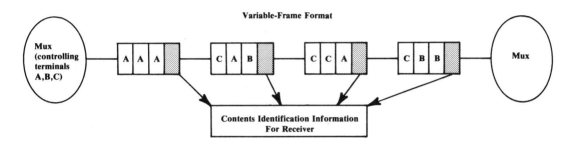

FIGURE 5-7
Fixed frame and variable frame TDM.

than an FDM. You are not reserving as much capacity for a terminal if it has nothing to send. This efficiency with respect to the channel capacity is the major advantage of time division multiplexing.

You will find it very easy to alter the number of TDM channels. If you start with 10 subchannels for your TDM, you do not have to buy a new mux if you want to increase to 20 subchannels. You simply buy the installation of another 10 subchannels for your mux.

One disadvantage of time division multiplexing stems from its major advantage—the use of frames. You cannot have multidrop operation with TDM. All frames remain intact until they are demultiplexed so they must terminate in one location. You cannot drop off one character of data from the frame at a location and then send the rest of the frame to another location.

Statistical Time Division Multiplexing (STDM).   Even when you use a time division bit mux, you still waste a large part of your available channel capacity. Most asynchronous terminals simply are not ready to transmit any data when the multiplexor is ready for it. Wasted channel capacity translates into wasted money, so engineers developed the statistical time division multiplexor (STDM, or stat mux).

STDMs allocate the available bandwidth to the terminals that have something to send and allocate no bandwidth to terminals that have nothing to send. In this way, no part of the bandwidth is wasted and the terminals that generate heavy traffic can have as much of the available transmission medium as they need. STDMs create frames for each transmission, and these have whatever length they need in order to accommodate the data the terminal is sending (Figure 5-8).

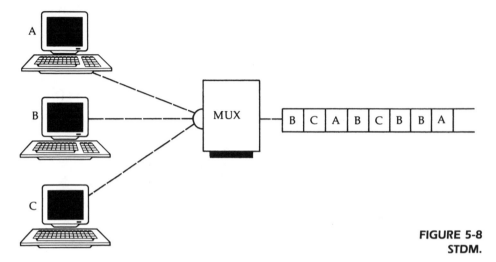

FIGURE 5-8
STDM.

If your data traffic occurs in bursts (called bursty traffic), you should consider a stat mux. An office with three Customer Service Representatives and one manager tied into one mux will produce bursty traffic. The three CSRs will generate many times the traffic that the manager will. If your business shows uniform traffic patterns, either uniformly high or uniformly low, the cheaper TDM solution will be the best one. As always, consider how your needs will evolve in the future.

Stat muxes need built-in memory and processing power in order to do their jobs. In a word, they need to be smart.

Smart Multiplexors.   In general, the word "smart" means "contains a microprocessor." A microprocessor is a CPU on a chip.

The microprocessor and associated memory means that smart muxes have storage and queueing facilities that standard muxes don't have. In order to qualify as "smart," a mux must be able to perform high-level logic functions, including code conversions (like ASCII to EBCDIC) and re-packaging of data (like a new data rate, or asynch to synchronous data).

Because they process communications traffic, you will also see smart muxes referred to as *communications processors*.

Concentrators.   Some manufacturers call their smart muxes *concentrators* because they concentrate traffic from several terminals into one efficient, high-volume data traffic line. Concentrators, like other smart muxes, have storage and queueing facilities.

You can think of a stat mux as a smart mux or a dumb concentrator, since it does a minimal amount of local processing. The differences between the simple mux and the smart mux are not clear-cut.

Communications Front Ends

Think of the modern office with its front office personnel. These workers screen calls, sort mail, route incoming people and messages to their proper destinations, and prevent congestion in the interior work areas by holding excess visitors in the front office.

A large computer's front-end processor provides similar services (Figure 5-9). Important but time-consuming tasks, such as handling data transmission to or from a network, are delegated to the front-end computer, freeing the larger computer for number-crunching and control functions.

A front-end processor can accomplish error-detection and correction, conversions (code, data rate, synchronization type, etc.), polls, multiplexing

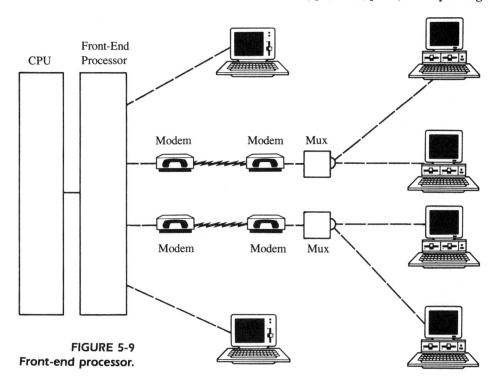

FIGURE 5-9
Front-end processor.

TABLE 5-1
Choosing a Multiplexor: TDM or FDM

If you:	If you:
Will not alter the number of channels	Will alter the number of channels
Will use multidrop lines	Will use only multipoint, never multidrop lines
No terminals produce significantly more traffic than others	Some terminals produce significantly more traffic than others
Efficiency not critical	Efficiency is critical
The absolutely least expensive solution is the only possible solution	Cost-benefit analysis may be allowed to dictate a higher priced solution
Then try:	Then try:
FDM	TDM or STDM

many terminal data lines into one data line for the computer, and can provide store-and-forward facilities. Store-and-forward is a special type of buffer that stores traffic from a busy line until it can be routed via an empty line.

Using Multiplexing

You can use muxes alone or as components of a network. Checklists later in this chapter will help you decide this issue.

For now, think about the driving force in mux development: efficient use of a single high-speed communications line by several low-speed devices. Multiplexors do their job with high reliability and no noticeable increase in response time. But the simple mux is not the only way to achieve efficiency.

When mapping a purchase strategy, ask yourself where in the communications system you want the traffic concentration to occur. At the port? At the mainframe host? Somewhere else? Table 5-1 will help you decide what type of multiplexing is best for your business.

WHAT A NETWORK IS

A *network* gives you two capabilities. The components can:

1. Share access to system resources, including disks and printers; and

2. Share information.

In simple form, you can get these two capabilities with the network imposters described in the previous section of this chapter. In order to qualify as a network, however, your system has to pass the third test: A network connects independent computers.

If your solution passes the first two tests but the components are not computers, you have a non-network distributed processing system. Any scheme where one computer controls a series of non-independent terminals cannot qualify as a network.

Each computer in a network can have its own operating system, internal clock, and other internal codes and operations. The component computers agree on the parameters of their common communications path and need not agree on anything else.

The OSI Model

Unclear thinking almost always stems from failure to clearly define objectives. When a program's logic looks like a bowl of spaghetti, when a speech or a report wanders randomly, you know that you don't have a clear objective or a clear path from where you are to where you want to be.

Network designers need clear objectives and a conceptual model for their work. Just as a well-designed program is designed in layers with interconnections but separate functions, a networking model would encapsulate specific functions at specific layers. Each level in the model would have clear tasks, clear goals, and clear inputs to the level above and the level below; and each level would do its own work without any attention to the internal workings of the other layers.

This model is the ISO/CCITT Open Systems Interconnection (OSI) model. The ISO published its first work on OSI in 1977, and in 1984, the CCITT approved and accepted the ISO's model. ISO called its model Open Systems Interconnection to emphasize that it would bring together equipment from many different manufacturers.

The OSI divides a network into seven layers of specific functions and capabilities, summarized in Table 5-2.

The layer boundaries allow information to flow horizontally (with protocols) and vertically (over interfaces). A protocol always connects two systems at the same layer, Layer 2 of one system with Layer 2 of another system, for example. An interface translates between layers (see Figure 5-10 on the following page).

The model ensures compatible connection and operation. Compatible connection means, just as it did with RS-232C, GPIB, and other interface standards, that devices from different manufacturers can be connected without causing electrical damage. This compatibility covers the physical and data link layers—the data path itself.

Compatible operation means that the components of your network can

TABLE 5-2
The OSI Levels

LEVEL	TASK
Physical	Transfers the bit stream to the communications channel
Data Link	Transfers data to its destination over the communications channel
Network	Routes data
Transport	Determines quality of service
Session	Coordinates interactions between users
Presentation	Converts codes, data formats, synchronization, and so on
Application	Supports application programs

actually cooperate to perform meaningful work. This is the job of the third to seventh layers.

These seven layers successfully encapsulate specific functions into neat little boxes. System designers need this sort of framework in order to create reliable order from the preexisting chaos. What does it all mean to you, as a business or personal computer user?

The ISO's Open Systems Interconnection model does not need to be universally implemented in order to be an enormous force for standardiza-

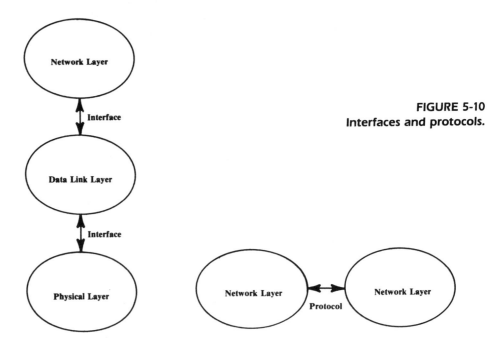

FIGURE 5-10
Interfaces and protocols.

tion in the industry. Even system designers who deviate from it at each level keep OSI at the front of their minds when designing their system.

We will now survey the seven OSI layers.

The Physical Layer

At the physical layer, you create a communication channel and transmit bits over it. The physical layer concerns itself with voltages and other electrical matters, not with how the data are packaged. The unit of exchange is the bit. The physical layer attaches no significance to bit patterns, not even to the number of bits in a byte. All these functions occur at higher layers. The voltage and signal compatibilities of RS-232-C, RS-449, GPIB, and CCITT's X.21 and V.24 belong to the physical layer.

To the extent that multiplexing, polling, handshakes, and other issues depend on electrical/physical media, they are involved in the physical layer.

The Data Link Layer

Bit patterns acquire meaning at this level. The data link layer's job includes data link protocols like SDLC and Bisync, protocol issues like ACK/NAK versus XON/XOFF, and data link issues contained in multiplexing, polling, multidrop and multipoint control, identification and sequencing of data, and formatting of blocks.

The unit of exchange is the frame. OSI's standard for this level is the High Level Data Link Control (HDLC), of which IBM's SDLC protocol is a subset.

HDLC allows every device to both send and receive, while SDLC insists that one device is the master or controller. OSI refers to this difference as balanced (HDLC) versus unbalanced (SDLC). "Unbalanced" refers to the power to send and receive in a SDLC system; one device controls all the others' interactions. In OSI's standard HDLC, power balances between the devices. Every device controls its own interactions with the outside world and is not controlled by any other device. All devices are co-equal as far as their right to use the communication facility is concerned.

The data link layer is the last level where hardware considerations are relevant. The upper layers of this scheme are all software.

Before we discuss these upper software layers, let's examine circuit, message, and packet switching.

Circuit and Message Switching. Do you remember the use of "switched" as a synonym for "voice-grade" when describing the telephone system? There are three types of switching: circuit, message, and packet switching (Figure 5-11).

The telephone system is an example of circuit switching. When you dial a number, you are asking the system to create a physical connection between your phone and the receiving phone. Another word for a physical connection over which electrical current flows is a *circuit*. The phone system creates this circuit by using thousands of switches.

The system must set up this communication channel in its entirety before communication begins, and the channel remains dedicated to the two (or more, on a conference call) users until they hang up their phones, physically ending the connection. The disadvantage of circuit switching is that an entire communication channel must remain dedicated to two users regardless of whether they actually need the full channel capacity for the entire time.

With message switching, there is no direct physical connection between the users. The *message* is sent to a switch that stores it and forwards it when convenient. An advantage of message switching is its ability to have multiple receivers. You can send the same message to several locations.

A circuit-switched system can become so bogged down with relatively low priority traffic that more important traffic is blocked, but a message-

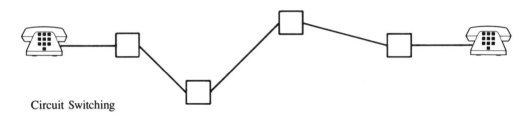

Circuit Switching

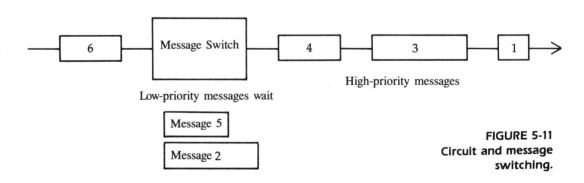

Low-priority messages wait

High-priority messages

FIGURE 5-11
Circuit and message switching.

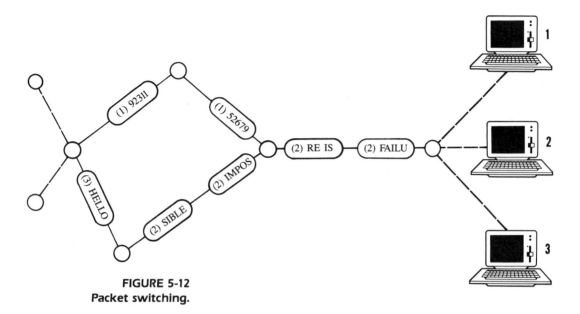

FIGURE 5-12
Packet switching.

switched system lets you assign a priority to each message. The most important messages get the system's attention, and lower priority messages wait until low load times. In a circuit-switched system, users don't know that a system is heavily loaded unless they are denied access totally. Error rates climb as the system becomes heavily loaded. In a message system, you can even out the load, keeping a fairly constant (and lower, on the average) error rate for all traffic.

Packet Switching.   Packet switching divides messages into chunks called *packets* (Figure 5-12). Your transmission line is not tied to one sender and receiver for very long. Each packet has control and identification information added to the data to allow the packet to arrive at its proper destination and be reassembled into a complete message when the other packets that make up the message arrive. The packet uses the communication channel only for as long as it needs the channel.

The Network Layer

The network layer creates and manages packets, the unit of transfer for this layer. The network layer's services include verification of packet receipt and details of packet routing. The CCITT's X.25 standard regulates how a DTE like your computer interacts with a packet-switched system, so it forms a standard for the network layer.

The service that the network layer provides for the transport layer falls into one of two conceptual models: the Virtual Circuit or the Datagram.

Virtual Circuit service creates a perfect, 100% error-free channel. You set up the connection, then transmit one or more packets and close down the connection. Once you start transmitting, you have a fixed sender and receiver. This means that you don't have to have destination information attached to each packet. It also means that all packets arrive at their destination in order. Virtual Circuit service is sometimes compared to telephone service: two devices communicate directly, with a point-to-point connection.

TABLE 5-3
Network Layer Service Options

1. Do you prefer to implement guaranteed service at the network layer or would you rather postpone Virtual Circuit service to the transport layer?

    Virtual Circuit service costs more than Datagram service. However, poorer quality (Datagram) service at the network layer means a higher, more expensive class of service at the transport layer.

2. Does your business require high-speed, realtime data traffic with no delays for error processing?

    You should use Datagram service at this layer and choose a higher class of service at the transport layer.

3. Do you need broadcast capability?

    You can use Datagram service to send the same message to more than one receiver.

4. Do you want packets to arrive in the order sent?

    If you choose Datagram service and packets arrive out of order, you will need more complex (and expensive) software in the upper layers to re-order the packets.

    With Virtual Circuit service at the network layer, packets will always arrive in the same order sent.

5. Do you need to reduce the cost of software at the transport layer?

    Virtual Circuit service at the network layer reduces the cost of the network/ transport interface.

Datagram service takes the messages that the transport layer uses and delivers each message individually so the messages arrive at their destinations in no particular order. Each Datagram contains complete destination information. An advantage of Datagram service is its ability to broadcast the same message to more than one receiver.

There are some situations in which Datagram service, clearly the more primitive solution, is the best solution. If your sender and receiver prefer high-speed data transfer without error control (particularly if error control involves retransmission and additional delay), Datagrams have an advantage. Any situation in which it doesn't matter whether packets arrive in order or not would benefit from Datagram service because you aren't paying for services that you don't need.

The question you ask yourself when deciding between the Virtual Circuit and the Datagram is where you want to control packet sequencing and errors. If the answer is the network layer, use Virtual Circuits. If the answer is the next higher layer, use Datagrams (see Table 5-3).

The network and higher layers are entirely software products. Above the data link layer, two devices do not communicate with each other over an actual physical medium. The protocols of layers 3 through 7 manage conceptual rather than physical data transfer. Since all that two machines ever exchange is a series of bits, only the physical and data link layers' protocols manage "real" data. But meaningful communication requires more than just the voltage compatibilities of the physical layer's RS-232-C, GPIB, and X.21. Meaningful communication will not occur without the protocols of layers 3 through 7, making these upper level protocols as important as the physical and data link layer protocols (Figure 5-13).

The Transport Layer

The transport layer names, addresses, buffers, and multiplexes messages, formed from the network layer's packets. The network layer also manages the establishment and termination of message transmission sessions.

The transport layer's chief object is to determine how a user can obtain the best possible service from the available facilities. There are five classes of service for error control:

0   Almost no error recognition and recovery.

1   Some error recognition and recovery.

2   Some error recognition and recovery, plus allowing multiplexing. If an error occurs at the network layer, the transport layer will inform you, then break off the communication.

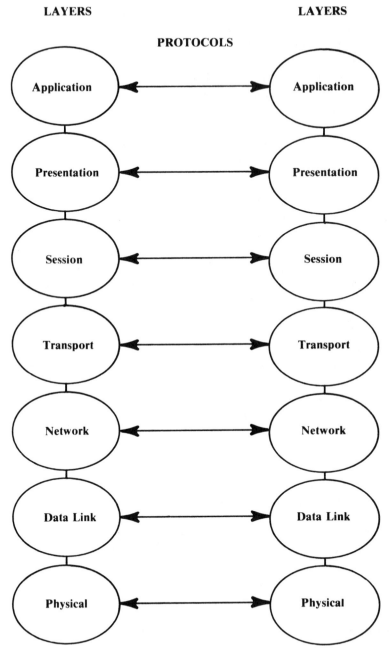

FIGURE 5-13
Conceptual and physical data transfer with
protocols.

3   Moderate level of error recognition and recovery. If an error occurs at the network layer, the transport layer will recover and proceed. You will not know that an error occurred. This option allows multiplexing.

4   Maximum level of error recognition and recovery. This class can detect and correct errors that stem from poor service at the lower levels. It will also recognize mis-ordered packets and put them in correct order.

The transport layer gives Virtual Circuit service. If the network layer of a particular system uses Datagram service, the transport/network interface must manage the transition from Datagrams to Virtual Circuits. Since Virtual Circuit service guarantees 100% reliability by imposing strict error control, Virtual Circuit service in the network layer lessens the transport layer's concern with error control. So Virtual Circuit service at the network layer frequently tandems with options 0, 1, and 2 above.

The Session Layer

The session layer adds services to what the transport layer provides by creating and managing sessions. The session layer creates and deletes the Virtual Circuits that the transport layer uses, and handles session crash recovery. If a transport layer error jeopardizes communications, the session layer recovers without informing the users, creating a new transport layer connection. It also authenticates and allows network access to users.

The type of connection—full-duplex or half-duplex—is another of the issues that the session layer resolves.

The Presentation Layer

The presentation layer concerns itself with network security, code translations, and format conversions. The file transfer protocol option defines how the system can move files from place to place in the system.

Another option for this layer is the virtual terminal protocol. Video terminals are remarkably non-standard devices. Because of the wide variety of ways that terminals handle such basics as input/output, terminal-handling would be a tremendous burden on a network's software. To remove this problem, the network communicates, not with the actual physical terminal, but with a logical device called the *virtual terminal*. This virtual terminal has set characteristics. The plethora of physical terminals from different manufacturers and the network's presentation layer software communicate with the virtual terminal instead of each other. The network is not burdened with the need to remember each terminal's specific parameters, and the network does not have to choose terminals from only one manufacturer. The different physical terminals with their specific strengths can all be part of the same local area network.

Networks create pipes and semaphores to implement the presentation layer's services. A network's *pipe* works like the conduits in your home, carrying a file instead of water or natural gas. A sender moves a file into the pipes area (usually on a hard disk) and creates a pipe to hold the file. The receiver taps into the pipe and the file gushes out. The network creates a pipe whenever it needs one, but the pipe disappears when the receiver reads the pipe. A pipe frequently translates the file from one operating system's format into another operating system's format. This is how different computers can share the information in files (Figure 5-14).

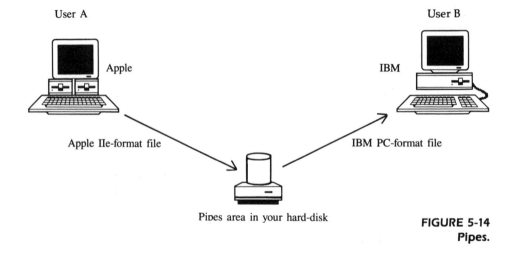

User A

Apple

Apple IIe-format file

User B

IBM

IBM PC-format file

Pipes area in your hard-disk

FIGURE 5-14
Pipes.

Semaphores constitute another mechanism for imposing order while allowing sharing. Just as a railroad semaphore bars access to the tracks when a train is approaching, the network's semaphores block access to other users when you are altering a file in some common memory area. Without these semaphores, the information-sharing of a network would be an invitation to chaos and mutual destruction.

The Application Layer

The application layer provides support for user programs. File managers, database managers, electronic mail, and other high-level network services work at this highest level.

TYPES OF NETWORKS

Of the three major schemes for dividing networks types, this section discusses two of them: architecture and bandwidth. The first major division—large scale versus local area networks—is the subject of Chapter 7.

Architecture

Each computer or other device in a network is called a *node*. The precise way you connect your nodes into a functioning system is a reflection of the network's architecture.

Architecture has implications for information-sharing. How is power shared among users in a particular architecture? Is there a direct link or a circuitous path between one node and another? How quickly does information travel? What kinds of security measures are possible? Is security easier or more difficult to implement on this architecture than on another? It would be difficult to overemphasize the importance of keeping these differences in information-sharing and power structure in mind when evaluating network architectures.

Star. The switchboard operator who connected customer calls by manually making physical connections between lines has a modern descendant, called a private automated branch exchange (PABX) or computerized branch exchange (CBX).

In a voice PABX, the main telephone number for the Ultimate Computer Co. is 732-8000. Mr. Smith's number is 732-8011, while Ms. Jones works at 732-8234. If Smith wants to reach Jones he dials 8234. Ultimate's private branch exchange routes all calls through the central switching station, but the delay this causes is noticeable only with very heavy traffic loads. If you purchase a PABX like Ultimate's, employees will dial each other's numbers without an operator's assistance.

You can have a local area network with this same star structure (Figure 5-15). In a star network, all messages pass through the central switching station in the center of the star. To qualify as a network, this central switch cannot have a controller/subordinate (or master/slave, in mainframe terminology) relationship with the nodes of the network.

The star network, either digital or voice/digital, varies from a simple, inexpensive solution to an extremely complex solution, depending on the services offered. Voice/digital integration in the modern office, discussed again in Chapter 8, produces the most complex but also the most interesting products. Table 5-4 lists the PABX services.

TABLE 5-4
The PABX Services

Call Forwarding	Set a phone to automatically switch calls to another phone, until further notice or until a specific time.
Camp on	Set a phone to "hold" an incoming call until the circuit is open. When the phone is free, the waiting circuit request immediately completes a circuit.
Call Waiting	The receiver hears a tone, repeating at a preset interval, alerting the receiver to the waiting call.
Auto Switch to Extension	The caller dials only the extension to reach another phone in the same network.
Auto Redial	One phone, upon reaching a busy number (outside of the network), automatically re-dials at a preset interval until an open circuit occurs. Then the calling phone rings and both caller and receiver pick up their phones.

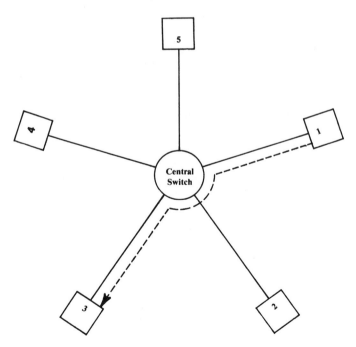

FIGURE 5-15
Star network.

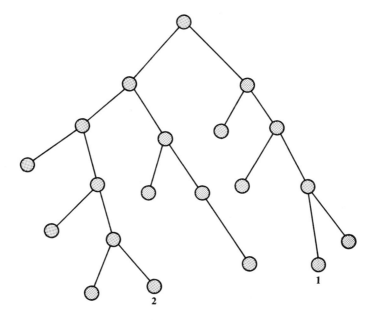

FIGURE 5-16
Tree network.

Tree.   A tree network makes information flow through branches. Any file system with directories forms a tree structure, as do most organizational charts (Figure 5-16).

In a tree network, information must pass along many branches and through many switches to move from one terminal node to another. To move from point 1 to point 2 in Figure 5-16, your data would have to travel through 8 switches. This can slow data traffic.

You can create functional groupings with a tree network. One branch could contain all the Account Receivable terminals, for example. The advantage of the tree structure stems from its ability to create these functional groupings, which also tend to isolate hardware problems. One branch can stop functioning without bringing down the entire network. So the hierarchical structure is both this architecture's greatest strength and its greatest liability.

Ring/Loop.   If your system places nodes in a closed loop or circle, your architecture is called a ring or loop (Figure 5-17). All addresses in the ring are sequential.

A ring can be unidirectional or bidirectional. A unidirectional ring moves traffic in only one direction. A bidirectional ring allows traffic to

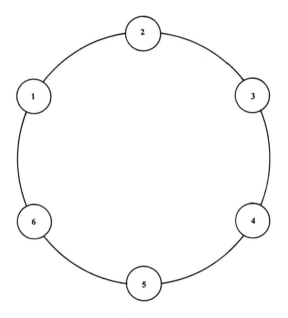

FIGURE 5-17
Ring network.

travel in either direction, although you can only move traffic in one direction at a time. A bidirectional ring can have faster transfer rates because node 1 can send data to node 6 without travelling past nodes 2 through 5.

Most rings implement control over the traffic with a token. The token is a bit pattern that means "permission to send." If a node with a ready data packet receives a token, it attaches the token to the packet and puts the combo on the network. The receiver sees its address, reads the data packet, marks it as having been read, and puts it back on the network. When the sender sees its packet with the "been read" notation in place, it removes the packet and releases the token. The token circulates to the next address in the list.

The ring architecture has some disadvantages compared to other architectures. You cannot add or subtract a node with as much ease as you can with a bus. The traffic must travel around the ring to each station in turn until it arrives at the proper address. This sets a practical upper limit on the size of the loop. Because data travels to each station in turn, you must have a plan for dealing with inactive stations. If you must remove one station in a ring for repair, you must have special bypass software or your entire network will shut down.

You will see more of the advantages and disadvantages of rings in Chapter 6, when we discuss local area network access methods.

Physical Star/Logical Ring.   This architecture forms a physical star but handles data like a ring (Figure 5-18).

The logical ring uses a token-passing control scheme, just as a physical

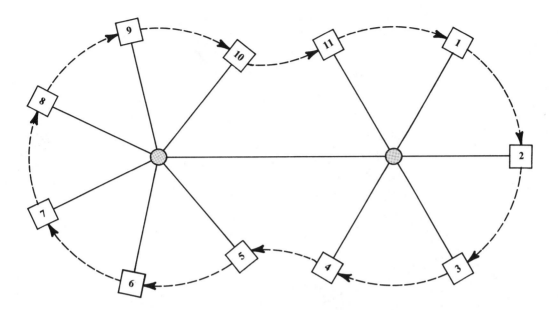

FIGURE 5-18
Physical star/logical ring network.

ring does. The token passes from address to address, giving each successive address permission to send. All data must travel through the central switch, as in any other star, but the logical ring does not allow the central switch to control the transactions.

This architecture combines the inexpensive nature of the physical star with the greater flexibility of a token-passing ring.

Bus. The bus in general and GPIB in particular were discussed in Chapter 3. The great advantage of the bus over other architectures is its non-hierarchical passive nature. Every device has the ability to communicate with every other device in the network.

You need not re-wire the entire network to add another node. Simply add your new station, then update the system list to include the new address. When your new, reconstituted network is ready, go back to work. If one station needs repair, it has no effect on the rest of the network.

Some buses use a token-passing scheme just as token rings do.

Complex Combinations. In addition to the simple types, complex network architectures abound. The mesh network connects every node with every other node, directly. Because of the complexity, this type of network has not become very popular.

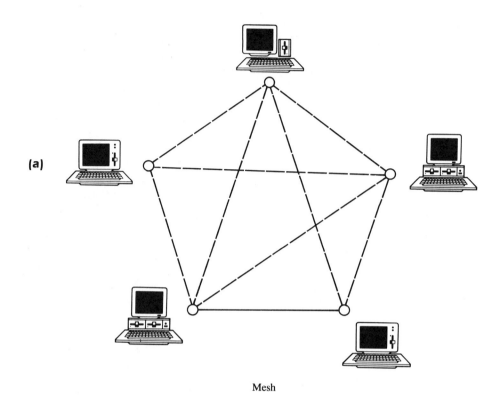

(a)

Mesh

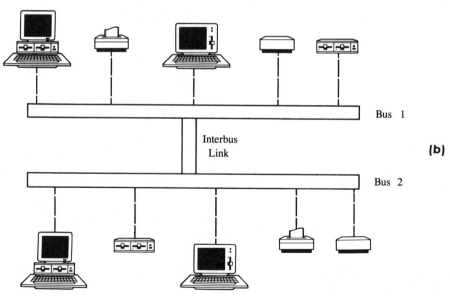

Bus 1

Interbus
Link

(b)

Bus 2

Multi-Bus

FIGURE 5-19
(a) Mesh networks and
(b) Multi-bus networks.

80

The multiple-bus architecture includes two or more buses connected by an inter-bus link called a bridge (Figure 5-19).

Since most single buses can support over 100 devices, the multi-bus does not enjoy a strong market push right now. It may well become more attractive in the future as computerization of the office continues.

Bandwidth

Your communications channel has a bandwidth, or range of possible frequency values. A wider bandwidth means that more information passes in any given time interval, in the same way that an eight-lane superhighway carries more traffic than a two-lane country road.

Any increase in bandwidth—particularly if the channel does not become physically large or unwieldy as a result—means more data moved and increased productivity. The major reason for today's furious level of research into fiber optics is the extremely large potential bandwidth for such a physically narrow medium.

Today's local area networks use either a baseband or a broadband medium. *Baseband*'s frequency range carries the data in its original form. *Broadband* carries information by impressing it on a carrier to lift it to the higher radio frequencies. Broadband gives you a broader band, hence the name. The broadband/baseband choice is one of the major topics included in Chapter 6.

The Network Decision

You now have all the background needed to make the first decision. Do you need a network?

Examine the spectrum from simple resource-sharing to a full-fledged

TABLE 5-5
A Spectrum of Capabilities

Less	Simple one-user operating system
↑	Multiprogramming operating system
	Simple mux
	Intelligent mux
	Combination of mux, port concentrator, front end
↓	Simple LAN (star or tree architecture)
More	Full-fledged LAN (ring, bus, mesh, combination architectures)

TABLE 5-6
Resource-Sharing: What Kind Do You Need?

Do you want to:	You need at least a:
Allow several users to use the same computational power?	Special operating system
Allow several users to use the same physical data traffic facility?	Mux, concentrator, etc.
Allow several users to share data, including files stored in different formats?	LAN

local area network in Table 5-5. Now work your way through the checklist in Table 5-6.

If you decide that a local area network fits your needs, Chapter 6 will help you choose a specific local area network.

6

local
area
networks

Imagine a busy office. One machine is receiving documents, including high-resolution multi-color images, from Chicago. Today's mail delivery includes documents now being fed directly into OCR scanners that will save the documents on floppy disks. No document, once put into a computer system anywhere in the world, ever needs to be retyped in this office.

You walk to your desk and listen to your voice mail, then read the electronic mail in your mailbox. You prepare replies quickly and request paper copies of the letter from San Francisco and the message from your chief assistant. Some of the messages you dictated to your computer's voice mail system last afternoon have already been acknowledged by the recipients. Other messages moved directly to word processing and await your signature. Your secretary's mailbox has a message from Accounting. They looked at Payroll's database and resolved the problem with your last expense check.

You walk down the hall to the Teleconferencing Center and spend the rest of the morning in a strategy meeting with sales managers in Boston, San Francisco, Los Angeles, and Dallas. You return to your office, dictate your meeting notes into your computer system, sign the letters, and go to lunch.

A dream? Yes, for now. But this dream rests on a series of local area networks.

A *local area network (LAN)* fulfills the three requirements of a network listed in Chapter 5 and does its work within a radius of 10 kilometers. (To be a network, a system must connect computers, share resources, and share information.) Ten kilometers, although not particularly "local" in other contexts, dwindles into insignificance when compared to the globe-spanning public packet networks of Chapter 7.

COMPONENTS OF LOCAL AREA NETWORK

The three major components of a LAN are the transmission medium (called the *path*), the devices, and the interfaces between the devices and the path (Figure 6-1).

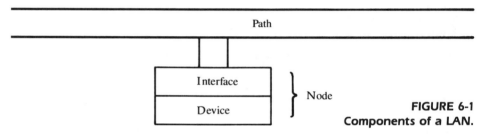

FIGURE 6-1
Components of a LAN.

The network interface, a hardware/software logical device, comes in two types. The intelligent interface includes buffers, packet assembly and disassembly (PAD) abilities, and other "intelligent" functions. An unintelligent interface makes the computer or another device perform these functions. The most popular LANs use an intelligent interface. The device plus its interface equals a network node or station.

Every device that attaches to and becomes part of a LAN must be a workstation, a server, or a gateway (Figure 6-2). A workstation—a network station where people work—means a computer connected to a network. *Gateways* connect your network to other networks and to mainframes and other resources. You will learn about gateways later in this chapter. Servers are the subject of the next section.

Servers

You can deliver certain services to the networked computers most efficiently by designating special purpose devices, called servers, to deliver these services. A *server,* either hardware or special software running on a

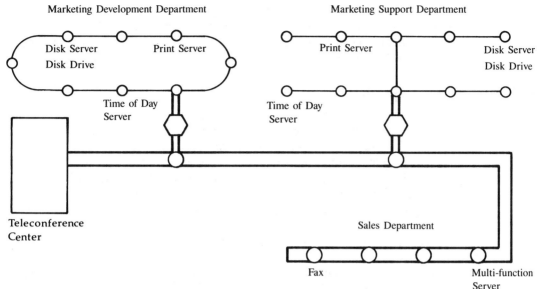

FIGURE 6-2
Facilities linked by LANs.

general purpose computer, provides services to clients. These clients can be servers themselves.

The server is the network designer's way of delegating responsibility for specific functions to specialists. A server does not work outside of its specialty, but it does its one job very well.

Look at Figure 6-2. Print servers give the network superior printer input/output. Disk servers make disk I/O as rapid and accurate as possible. File servers give superior service to the disk server or any other network resource that accesses files. The Time-of-Day server gives the network its time-of-day clock.

A network with electronic mail servers and communications servers would have more efficient mail and communications. Beyond the mid-1980s, gateway servers, database servers, and more efficient electronic mail servers will be standard network components.

ACCESS METHODS

An *access method* describes how the devices share the transmission facility in a network. Do stations transmit only in numerical order of their logical addresses? Does a station contend for an open path, depending on speed to grab the facility before its rivals, as a player vies to snatch the basketball as soon as it leaves the referee's hands?

Choosing the best access method for your business requires an accurate and comprehensive look at present and projected data traffic patterns. You will find checklists in this section to help you ask the right questions when you consider an access method.

Token-Passing

One of the main access choices, token-passing, received a brief treatment in Chapter 5. In some systems, the station with the token can only send one packet of data regardless of what its needs may be, while other systems allow a station to send everything that's waiting in its buffer.

Manufacturers combine the token-passing access method with different architectures, primarily rings and buses. Remember in this discussion that the access method handles data in accordance with the logical architecture. If a network is a physical star but a logical bus, think of it as a bus because it will handle its data as a bus does.

In a ring system with every station active, each station receives and then regenerates the *token,* the bit pattern 11111111. When a station wishes to add a data packet to the token, it regenerates the token as the bit pattern 11111110. The new bit pattern, called a connector, alerts all listeners to the fact that a data packet follows it (Figure 6-3). In effect, this situation differs from hub go-ahead polling only in that no controller sends out polls.

One location will see its address in the destination part of the packet's

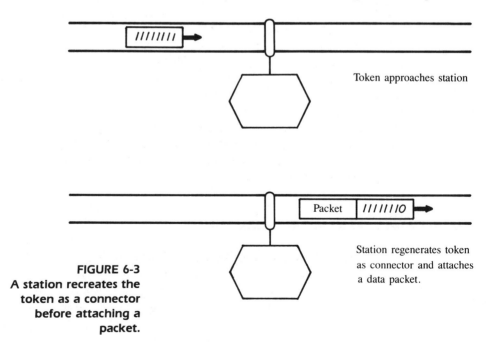

Token approaches station

Station regenerates token as connector and attaches a data packet.

FIGURE 6-3
A station recreates the token as a connector before attaching a packet.

control information. When it regenerates the packet, it changes one position in the packet's control field, the "I've been read" position. When the source receives the connector and data packet and sees that the receiver has read the packet, it does not regenerate the data packet. It turns the connector back into a token by changing the final 0 to a 1. The network is now free for new traffic.

The token-passing scheme has one powerful advantage. Every station knows that, regardless of how busy the network becomes, it will receive the token within a certain predetermined maximum time. In a token-passing scheme, no two or more devices will attempt to use the data channel at the same time. Any device that receives permission to proceed knows that it has undisputed rights to the channel for a specific time period. Some applications require that every station be guaranteed access within a certain maximum time limit. Process control, medical monitoring, and other realtime applications need token-passing for this reason.

Token-passing has some disadvantages, including the delay while a token circulates. No station can transmit until it changes the token to a connector. If the token is passing station 3 while station 20 has a data packet ready, the ready station must wait until the token reaches it. During those microseconds, the network's capacity is completely wasted. The larger the network, the greater the delay and inefficiency with token-passing.

Token-passing rings usually require active stations. If any station goes down, the entire network collapses because each station must regenerate the data packet or token. To eliminate this risk, you need bypass software that will automatically reroute traffic past a dead node.

The major disadvantage of token-passing remains the same for any architecture: What do you do about lost or garbled tokens? In some systems, a station can regenerate the token if it hasn't seen a token for a preset period of time. That should solve the problem. But in order to keep power decentralized, every station must have this ability. What happens if more than one station creates a token? Absolute chaos results.

Slotted Ring

The slotted ring, with some of the characteristics of the token-passing ring, has not been embraced by many manufacturers. Instead of passing a token, the slotted ring divides itself into areas, called slots, which circulate. When an empty slot passes it, a station can place a data packet into the slot. The control field of the data packet includes the destination's address. When the receiver sees its address, it reads the data packet, changing the packet's "I've been read" status. When the sender sees that the packet has been read, it will remove it and leave the slot empty once more. Every one of the slots can carry data packets, making this an efficient ring option (Figure 6-4).

Because slots have a set size, you cannot use variable-sized packets with

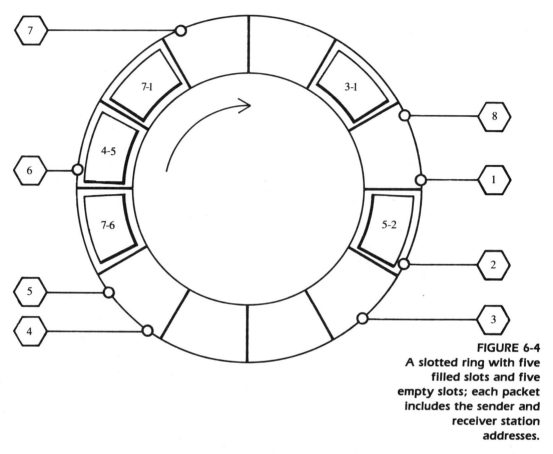

FIGURE 6-4
A slotted ring with five
filled slots and five
empty slots; each packet
includes the sender and
receiver station
addresses.

a slotted ring. Another disadvantage slotted rings share with token-passing is that the packets continue to circulate (and take up channel capacity) until the sender sees that the packet has been read.

Contention: CSMA

Contention does not guarantee access and does not require a station to receive permission before it starts transmitting. Many stations contend for the same transmission medium.

Contention in the bus architecture most commonly uses *carrier sense multiple access (CSMA)*. A station with a data packet to send tests the path. If it doesn't sense a carrier from another station, it sends the packet.

Approximately 95% of the time (under average load conditions), the packet reaches its destination without mishap. However, if a second station puts a packet on the path while the first packet is using it, the packets may *collide* (Figure 6-5).

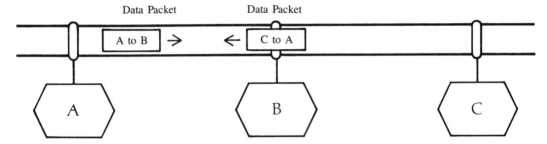

FIGURE 6-5
Two packets preparing to collide.

The possibility of collisions means that each network has a minimum required packet size that depends on the physical size of the network. If packets are too small relative to the time it takes a packet to travel from one end of the network to another, collisions would not be detected.

System designers have developed many strategies for avoiding or coping with CSMA's collisions. Most manufacturers use a variant of either collision detect (CD) or collision avoid (CA). With collision detect, a station transmits as soon as it sees an empty path. It continues to monitor the path, and if it detects a collision (the electrical characteristics of the medium change when a collision occurs), it transmits a jam signal (Figure 6-6). The jam alerts all the other receivers, and the senders cut short their packets.

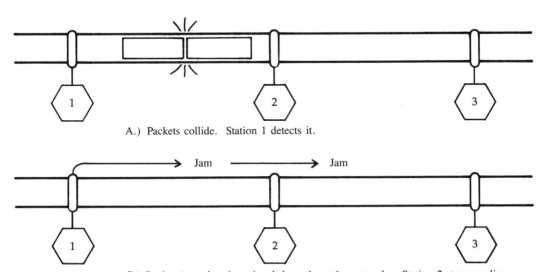

FIGURE 6-6
CD's jam signal cuts short a collision.

The CD strategy includes an inevitable delay in packet transmission, which accounts for many collisions. The network interface tests the path, and if it finds an empty path, it tells the computer to send its data. The interface creates a packet and places it on the path some microseconds after it tested the path. (All these events occur in microseconds and fractions of a microsecond.) Another station could put a packet on the path between the time a station tests the path and the time it actually transmits the packet.

Collision avoidance attempts to eliminate this problem by requiring the network interface unit to test the path twice: initially as CD does, then again just before it places the data packet on the path.

CA does not need a jam signal to alert all stations to the collision because the senders do not stop sending as soon as they detect the collision. The two packets continue to collide until both entire packets have been transmitted. This long collision effectively alerts all stations. Since CA makes collisions less likely to occur in the first place, its efficiency is not lower than CD even though it doesn't cut its collisions short.

Collision detection and avoidance strategies have received a great deal of attention because "collision" sounds very dramatic. However, the average contention LAN uses only 5–10% of its capacity. A heavily loaded network uses 50% of its capacity. Before the 40% level, collisions have a negligible effect on your system's performance.

The deaf state poses another potential problem. When your network interface unit is busy interacting with your computer, it's not monitoring the path. A packet that arrives during this "deaf" time is a lost packet. (When the sender does not receive an ACK or other acknowledgement character, it will resend the packet.) Some sophisticated network products, like the Intel 82586 communications co-processor discussed later in this chapter, can eliminate the deaf state.

CSMA systems must also have a mechanism for defeating the queueing problem. After a collision occurs, if the potential senders wait the same amount of time and then try again, the packets will collide again. Manufacturers have developed various ways to manage this queue of contenders. Most strategies involve requiring the stations to wait random amounts of time before transmitting. This prevents two or more stations from transmitting at the same time once again. Because possession of the path is up for grabs every time a packet reaches its destination, the stakes are high for each contending station.

Contention Ring

Manufacturers' contention schemes center on rings and buses, just as the token-passing schemes do. The contention ring uses the basic contention idea under light, bursty traffic conditions and becomes a token-passing ring when traffic is heavy and collisions occur. When traffic is light, a station with data simply begins transmitting as soon as it sees that the path is empty. It attaches a token to the end of the data packet. If two stations put packets on what they consider an empty ring, the packets may collide. Each station waits, then tries again. Under high load conditions, when collisions would be frequent, the stations do not transmit until they receive a token.

The contention ring puts the advantages of contention and token-passing into an interesting mix.

Choosing an Access Method

Contention schemes don't waste capacity because no token circulates past stations that have nothing to send, while other stations with data packets must wait. With a contention scheme, a station's access is statistical (like a statistical mux), while token-passing gives you deterministic access (like frequency division or time division multiplexing).

In general, bursty traffic benefits from contention while uniform traffic or heavy traffic in general works better with a slot or token-passing scheme. If you want CSMA and expect periodic heavy traffic, you must keep CA's and CD's particular advantages in mind. With collision avoidance, collisions will be less likely to occur, but a jam will not cut the collisions short. Table 6-1 compares access methods.

TABLE 6-1
Access Methods

TOKEN-PASSING RING	SLOTTED RING	CSMA
Deterministic	Statistical	Statistical
Access guaranteed in a specific time period.	Access guaranteed when traffic is heavy.	No guarantee of access.
Wasted capacity while token circulates.	No wasted capacity.	No wasted capacity.
Packet must return to sender before medium is free.	Packet must return to sender before medium is free.	Medium is free as soon as packet arrives. Receiver must ACK or sender resends packet.
Lost token problem.	Slots cannot be lost or garbled. Packets cannot collide.	Access based on sense; packets can collide.

TRANSPORT LAYER SERVICES IN YOUR LOCAL AREA NETWORK

We must delve into some particular transport layer services in more detail before we can look at how a LAN works.

The Socket

The transport address is a memory location that determines what the network interface will do with packets. The alternate name, socket, may be more descriptive, since it "plugs" the interface into the network.

A *socket* is an address that receives the packet. The packet splits into message and control fields, then the message moves to its correct destination in the receiving computer's memory. Specifically, the message arrives at the correct process (Figure 6-7). For every active process, there is a transport address or socket.

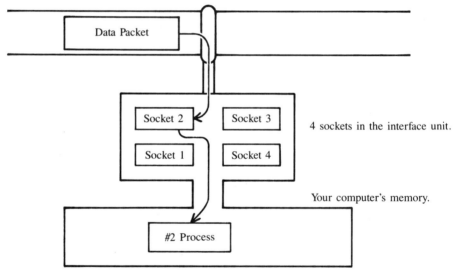

FIGURE 6-7
A data packet goes to a socket and then to the process.

The socket must be unique in order to do its job. The CCITT recommends a 14-digit address. The first 4 digits identify the particular segment or section of the network. The next 10 digits identify the network station and the unique socket within it.

Gateways and Internetworking

On its own, your LAN will give you powerful information and resource-sharing. But you need more than that to accomplish the tasks listed at the start of this chapter. In order to connect your local area network to other LANs and to public packet networks, private vendor networks and message-handling systems, independent databases, videotex services, and other resources, you need a gateway.

The name gateway describes its functions very well. With a sophisticated gateway, you can forget about compatibility and protocols and every other nightmare involved in trying to communicate directly with the mainframe or other network. Your LAN sees the gateway simply as an address to which packets are routed and from which other packets emerge. The gateway appears to each network as simply another node. Neither network has to change its own internal operations to conform with the other, in the same way that the United Nations uses translators rather than imposing one standard language on the world (Figure 6-8).

FIGURE 6-8
A gateway acts as a translator and repackager of data packets.

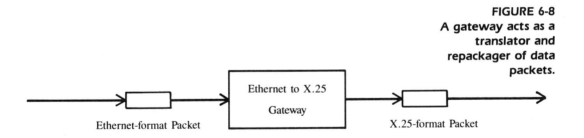

Ethernet to X.25 Gateway

Ethernet-format Packet   X.25-format Packet

Gateways come in different types, with different capabilities. Some simple gateways can only connect two networks of the same type. More sophisticated gateways connect networks using different architectures, media, and protocols. With a gateway, broadband and baseband networks communicate with each other. (You will see broadband and baseband networks later in this chapter.) You can also buy gateways to connect your LAN to a private network or mainframe. For example, your LAN could communicate with an SNA network through a gateway. (SNA is IBM's mainframe-oriented network.) Figures 6-2 and 6-9 show LAN gateways.

The networks of the late 1980s will depend more heavily on gateways. With gateways, local networks can link together to form metropolitan area and even larger networks and can connect to computer resources anywhere in the world.

The most important reason for the gateway excitement comes from a gateway's ability to let microcomputer and microcomputer local area net-

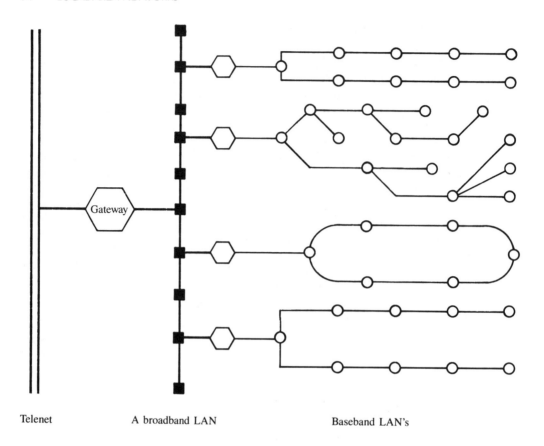

Telenet   A broadband LAN   Baseband LAN's

FIGURE 6-9
Gateways connect
networks with different
architectures and media.

work owners stop spending so much time dealing with compatibility problems. Specifically, the LAN and microcomputer owners will substantially reduce their expenditures for software that helps them conform to another system's needs. With high-level gateways, you can completely ignore every other system's needs and concentrate on your own. The potential of these sophisticated gateways is nothing short of breathtaking. (At present, most gateways convert only up to the Network Layer. With this simple type of gateway, you do have to consider the compatibility of the upper levels.)

Chapter 7 will include the current standards work on X.75, the CCITT's internetworking standard.

STANDARDS

All the various standards organizations—national, regional and international—have worked on the question of local area network standardization. The most influential group of standards was developed by the IEEE and approved by the ISO.

The IEEE LAN Committee Standards

The IEEE's Local Area Network (802) Standards Committee, unable to develop one standard architecture/access method combination, developed three standards. The three standards, named 802.3, 802.4, and 802.5, standardize three popular combinations. Having three "standards" may seem a contradiction in terms, but to some extent the failure of consensus was inevitable with the explosion of products and manufacturers in the LAN market.

The 802.3 subcommittee developed a CSMA/CD bus standard, while 802.4 and 802.5 produced the token-passing bus and token-passing ring standards. The 802.3 CSMA/CD bus standard is very similar to Ethernet, one of the products profiled later in this chapter.

The 802.4 token-passing bus passes a token from address to address in a master list (Figure 6-10).

The 802.5 token-passing ring standard (Figure 6-11) conforms very closely to IBM's LAN product, which uses twisted wire pair and duplex optical fiber cable.

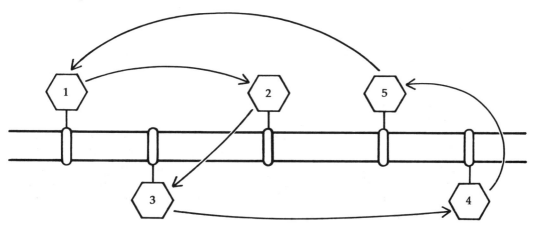

FIGURE 6-10
The token-passing bus.

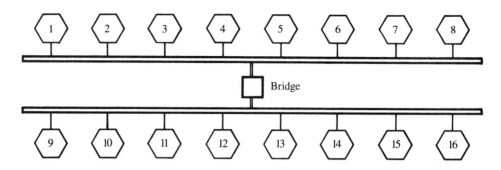

FIGURE 6-11
Two token-passing rings linked by a bridge
form one network.

The 802.6 standard specifies a network covering a metropolitan area. Because a metropolitan area can cover 10 kilometers or less, 802.6 qualifies as part of the IEEE's 802 family.

All these standards—802.3 through 802.6—standardize the physical layer's requirements, and manufacturers are working to create products that comply with them. IEEE's 802.2 standard specifies a logical link control protocol for the Data Link Layer for all architecture/access combinations.

The ISO approved the IEEE 802 Committee's standards in 1984.

MEDIA ISSUES

You must consider a proper medium for your LAN. In a few cases, the architecture you choose will restrict your choice of medium, but you can mix media with architecture and access methods relatively independently.

The simplest and generally least expensive medium—the cable containing a twisted-wire pair—installs easily. If you can install a stereo system, you can install twisted-pair cable. You can subtract and move network stations easily with no loss of signal strength. As the oldest LAN medium, it has proven its reliability.

Coaxial (coax) cable contains a conducting wire surrounded by insulating material. The networks that use coax claim greater reliability and less interference than with twisted-wire cable, and some scientific studies back up this claim. Other studies do not show a difference. If a difference exists at all, it's not significant. Coax's ease of installation and expansion almost equal that of twisted-wire cable.

A form of radio transmission, microwave is becoming more popular as a LAN medium for applications stretching beyond one building. Microwave can pack many more voice channels than an ordinary wire cable but

FIGURE 6-12
A Racon microwave transmitter on the rooftop
in the foreground transmits packets to the
receiver on the main building of City National
Bank. (Photo courtesy of Racon, Inc., Seattle,
Wash.)

transmission must always be along the line-of-sight; transmitters must be able to "see" each other. Some large companies and universities use microwave technology to substitute for cables between the buildings of a multi-building LAN. Unfortunately, microwaves offer no more security from interception than the traditional transmission media do—which is to say, none at all (Figure 6-12).

Fiber optics, the most promising new technology, can give you data transfer rates of up to 1 gigabits per second (1 billion bps) with a physically narrow medium. Each fiber, composed of a glass material, connects to a light-emitting diode (LED) or laser that generates a carrier. The signal modulates the light carrier and the photodiode at the receiving end of the cable turns the information back into an analog or digital signal. Each cable contains several optical fibers. The U.S. telephone system uses fiber optic cables for some of its high-speed lines.

Fiber optics has other advantages beyond its high data rates. The fiber optic cable itself, very difficult to tap, contributes to the network's security. The confined signal does not cause interference to nearby devices. Nor will it accept interference, being almost impervious to lightning and other meterological phenomena, impulse noise, electromagnetic interference (EMI), radio-frequency interference (RFI), and cross-talk. The fiber optic

TABLE 6-2
LAN Media

MEDIUM	MAX. DATA TRANSFER RATE (bps)	MAX. DISTANCE (km)
Twisted Wire	50–60 K	1
Coax (baseband)	50 M	1–3
Coax (broadband)	350 M	10
Fiber Optics	1 G	10

K = Kilobits/sec.   M = Megabits/sec.   G = Gigabits/sec.

cable has the advantages of light weight, flexibility, and a much thinner diameter than other cables. Lastly, if you need to use a LAN in a combustible area, fiber optic cables cannot create the short circuits that introduce fire hazards.

Fiber optics has some disadvantages, of course. The signal weakens with each new station added to the system so the cable needs power boosters at regular intervals. The process of installation and the process of adding additional stations to the network require much more technical expertise than coax or twisted-wire pair cable. Finally, fiber optics gives you very limited multidrop capability. Table 6-2 compares fiber optics, coax (broadband), coax (baseband), and twisted-wire.

The final network technology, satellite transmission, never connects the components of a local area network. It takes a significant amount of time by LAN standards for a packet to travel from the transmitting antenna to the receiving antenna via a satellite in a geosynchronous 37,200 kilometer-high orbit. Because of this signal propagation delay, CSMA and token-passing are unfeasible.

First used only as a cable-in-the-sky, giving point-to-point connections as cable does, satellites are now more and more used as broadcasters, transmitting packets over a wide area. The receivers collect their packets from the broadcast stream (Figure 6-13). (Packets always have destination information attached to them, so receivers always know which packets belong to them.) The receivers can be LANs and large-scale networks.

The major disadvantage of satellite transmission stems from its major advantage. Because of its broadcast nature, satellite transmissions are very easy to pirate unless the sender takes precautions that we'll discuss in Chapter 9.

FIGURE 6-13
Earth station collects packets from an orbiting
satellite. (Photo by V. Marney-Petix)

Choosing a Medium

The medium is one of the factors you'll evaluate when you are studying a particular vendor's LAN offering. Twisted-wire pair cable and coax have the advantage of easy installation and expansion. Other media, particularly fiber optics, will give you more capabilities, but you'll pay more in costs and in more difficult installation and expansion.

The checklist in Table 6-3 will help you keep the pros and cons of each medium in mind.

THE BASEBAND/BROADBAND DECISON

Most of what we have discussed up to now concerning "networks" actually refers to baseband systems. Whatever medium it uses—either twisted-wire pair, fiber optics, or coax cable—baseband gives you only one data channel. With token-passing, slots or contention, the only resource you have for data transfer is this single channel. The digital data travel on a passive medium,

TABLE 6-3
Choosing a Medium

	(check)
1. Must it be simple to install or very rugged?	☐
2. Do you need the highest possible data transfer rate?	☐
3. Do you need to couple inexpensive installation with distances up to 1 kilometer?	☐
4. Do you need to couple inexpensive installation with distances from 1 to 10 kilometers?	☐
5. Must you reduce fire hazards in the workplace?	☐
6. Do you want ease of adding, subtracting, and moving workstations?	☐
7. Do you have a large area to connect?	☐
8. Do you need high security from wiretaps and other assaults on the physical medium?	☐
9. Will you use a star architecture?	☐
10. Will you use a token-passing ring or a CSMA/CD bus?	☐
11. Do you need multidrop capability?	☐
12. Do you need better than average freedom from radio-frequency (RFI) and other (EMI) interference, or lightning-caused power surges?	☐

If you chose 1, 3, 6, 9, 10, and 11	Consider twisted-wire cable.
If you chose 1, 4, 6, 9, 10, and 11	Consider baseband coax.
If you chose 2, 5, 8, 12, and 9 or 10	Consider fiber optics.
If you chose 7 but not 9	Consider a microwave link for the inter-building part of your data path.

which means that although individual nodes may fail, the network transmission medium itself rarely fails.

Broadband is very different. The bandwidth divides into an inbound band and an outbound band, with a guard band to separate them (Figure 6-14). The inbound band carries data from the network nodes to the headend. An analog translation device, the headend takes the data con-

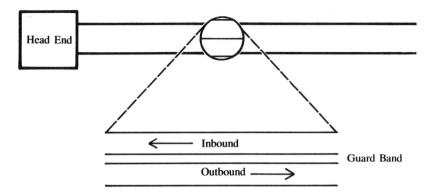

FIGURE 6-14
Inbound and outbound
traffic separated by a
guard band.

tained in the inbound band's channels and broadcasts it on the outbound band. All nodes send their data on the inbound band and listen for their address on the outbound band.

Broadband's two bands divide into data channels. Each channel can carry a different type of data, including voice and video, at a different data rate. Each type of traffic must have its own channel: you cannot multiplex voice mail traffic with video signals and computer data traffic.

Broadband's architecture is logical bus/physical tree, particularly suited to multidrop operation. Branching tree architecture also allows you to isolate electrical and physical layer problems in one branch, keeping the rest of the network up and running.

The usual solution gives you complete transmission access to other nodes on your same branch. On different channels of the same cable (using the same headend), a store-and-forward packet gateway routes packets from one channel to another. These internal gateways, called bridges (Figure 6-15), are the structures you first saw in Chapter 5 as part of the multi-bus architecture. Your traffic contends for space on the particular channel of the inbound band of its cable by using CSMA.

Broadband Technology

A broadband network contains a path, devices, and interfaces. In keeping with the definition of interface, you would expect a network interface unit to translate something for the network. In this case, the interface unit contains or works with an RF (radio-frequency) modem, which takes a device's data and translates it to radio frequencies of the

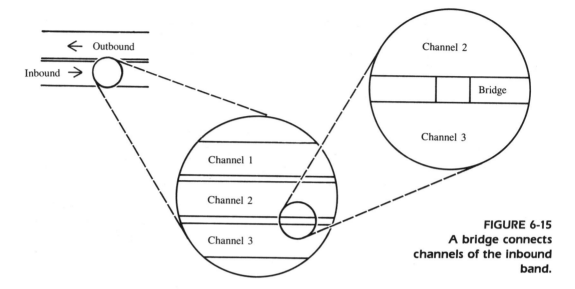

**FIGURE 6-15
A bridge connects
channels of the inbound
band.**

inbound band. The network interface unit packetizes digital data into analog radio frequency signals (Figure 6-16).

A broadband network uses the same standard, easily obtainable cable that cable TV (CATV) uses, carrying data in analog form at the radio frequencies. Because this cable is an active medium, the transmission medium itself can fail, stalling the entire network. The radio-frequency (RF) modems that broadband requires need careful calibration and frequent (for a modem) adjustments. The cable plant can also require adjustment.

Broadband's advantages—wide bandwidth, multiple channels, and higher data transfer rates—include costs in addition to a higher price tag. A

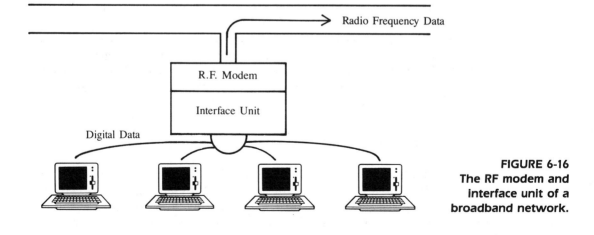

**FIGURE 6-16
The RF modem and
interface unit of a
broadband network.**

broadband network is more difficult to design, maintain, and expand than a typical baseband network.

Broadband Standards

Since they developed from the CATV industry, broadband standards concern themselves with channel widths, channel separation, activity of the headend, and other frequency related matters.

The IEEE 802 Committee is developing recommendations that will cover broadband media issues. The greatest bar to international broadband standardization is the channel width. A U.S. channel, 6 MHz (megahertz) wide, does not equal Europe's 8-MHz channels.

Broadband Solutions

The two networks profiled in this section are strong sellers and represent the most common broadband technology.

Each network uses CSMA/CD to share a channel, along with FDM or TDM. Both manufacturers use an open architecture, designed to accept devices from different manufacturers.

Each network uses an intelligent network interface unit that uses several buffers and manages PAD, Virtual Circuit service, error control, flow control, protocol, and code conversions. These network interface units provide partial implementations of the top six layers of the OSI model.

Both networks have provisions for internetworking, including bridges to other networks by the same manufacturer and gateways to baseband local area networks, public packet networks, and mainframe-oriented computer networks.

Net/One.   Net/One, produced by Ungermann-Bass of Santa Clara, California, uses 59.75–89.75 MHz for its inbound band and 252–282 MHz for its outbound band. These bands carry up to 5 channels at a data rate of up to 5 Mbps.

A Net/One network can include devices no more than 5 miles (8 km) from a headend, which includes a Channel Translator. Your data will have no more than a 17-km round trip.

The Net/One network interface unit—called a Network Interface Unit (NIU)—includes an RF modem and can connect up to 24 devices conforming to any one of the following standards: IEEE 488 (GPIB) parallel, RS-232-C serial, RS-449 serial, or V.35 serial. Each Channel Translator can handle up to 300 NIUs per channel, and there are 5 channels available. This gives a maximum device capacity of 36,000 devices (300 $\times$ 24 $\times$ 5).

You can configure an NIU to operate on Ethernet baseband and fiber optic cable as well as broadband cable. Bridges allow Net/One networks using different media to communicate together, and allow you to create networks that are larger than the capacity of any one medium.

Net/One's installed base includes over 500 complete networks and 6000 nodes.

LocalNet.   LocalNet, produced by Sytek, Inc., of Mountain View, California, has an inbound band at 40–106 MHz and an outbound band at 196–262 MHz.

LocalNet's System 20 gives you 128 Kbps capacity channels suitable for low-speed, low-traffic devices, like most personal computers. The maximum one-way distance to the headend, called Tverter, must be under 50 kilometers (35 miles). Devices use a serial interface, either synchronous or asynchronous.

LocalNet's network interface unit, called a Packet Communication Unit (PCU), includes an RF modem. A complete network can include 20,000 devices.

LocalNet's installed base tops 500 networks, with 55,000 nodes.

Baseband Solutions

Both networks use the CSMA contention bus, with Omninet choosing CA and Ethernet choosing CD, and both use an intelligent network interface unit.

Omninet.   The clear industry sales leader, Omninet is produced by Corvus Systems, Inc., of San Jose, California.

Omninet avoids the queueing problem by using an exponential backoff algorithm. This means that, after a collision occurs, each sender waits a random amount of time before testing the path. The amount of time that they "backoff" before trying again increases exponentially as traffic becomes heavier and collisions occur more frequently. Omninet puts its contention strategy (CA) in firmware (software permanently burned onto a chip) that executes almost as quickly as hardware.

Omninet carries up to 1 Mbps over segments of up to 300 meters, serving 64 stations. Repeaters can lengthen the network to 1.2 kilometers (4000 feet).

Omninet's intelligent network interface, called a transporter, implements the first four layers of the OSI model—hence the name. Composed of hardware and software, the transporter takes a device's data and packetizes it, then transmits it. Each transporter can have up to four sockets (Figure 6-17).

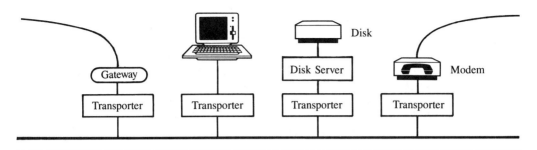

FIGURE 6-17
Transporters connect devices to Omninet.

The transporter cuts down on the amount of buffer space it needs by using direct memory access (DMA). With DMA, the transporter bypasses the computer's memory management, reaching directly into the computer's memory with its own control logic. One DMA cycle can follow immediately after another, with reaches to unrelated areas of memory. DMA increases the speed of memory access, but of course a defective transporter could wreak havoc in memory because it bypasses some of the computer's safety mechanisms. Other networks also use DMA to increase speed.

One of the transporter's components is the Advanced Data Link Controller (ADLC), which handles the collision avoidance strategy at the Data Link layer. The Message Header field includes:

■ Destination or station address

■ Source address

■ Destination socket

■ Number of times the message has been retransmitted, beginning with 0 on the first transmission

■ Length of the User Control and User Data fields that follow

■ Parity bit (½). Combined with the retransmission field, this alerts the receiver to duplicate packets.

Omninet's packets include an optional User Header field, which the transporter strips away from incoming packets and routes into a separate area of its memory. The standard Omninet Header field includes the socket number.

Faced with the Datagram versus Virtual Circuit decision, Corvus decided to find a third alternative for Omninet and called it the Reliable Datagram. The one-way, transaction-oriented Datagram does not provide enough service for most applications, but Virtual Circuit service at the network layer needs more memory than could be put into a transporter without leading to an unacceptable increase in complexity (and price). The Reliable Datagram has the most necessary features of the Virtual Circuit, including requiring that every message be received correctly. Reliable Datagram service discards duplicate packets, and all packets arrive in the same order they were sent, as with normal Datagram service.

Constellation II software offers a partial implementation of layers 5–7 of the OSI. Since the upper OSI layers are service-oriented, the software that implements it is service-oriented. Constellation II manages network resource-sharing, particularly the work of the different servers and the interaction of the different operating systems through the pipes area of the hard disks. Omninet's disk servers will serve up to four Winchester disks, as shown in Figure 6-2.

Omninet has 5000 networks installed, supporting 40,000 nodes. Its twisted-wire pair cable helps make it the most popular low-cost solution.

Ethernet.   Ethernet began as a prototype product developed by Xerox Corporation of Stamford, Connecticut. Before Xerox completed development, Digital Equipment Corporation of Maynard, Massachusetts, and Intel Corporation of Santa Clara, California, joined as backers. This cooperation

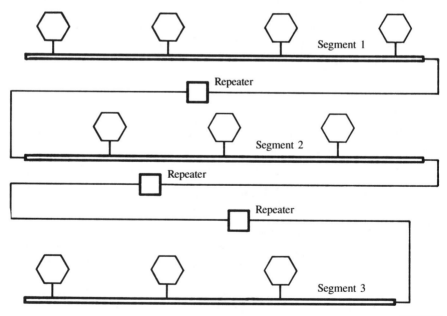

FIGURE 6-18
Ethernet network with repeaters.

by three industry powerhouses gave Ethernet a tremendous boost. The IEEE 802.3 CSMA/CD bus standard corresponds very closely to Ethernet.

Ethernet implements its collision detection in hardware; it uses an exponential backoff algorithm just as Omninet does.

An Ethernet network carries data at a maximum rate of 10 Mbps. A segment can be up to 500 meters (1625 feet), expandable to 2.3 kilometers (7600 feet) with repeaters, and can hold up to 1024 nodes (Figure 6-18). Ethernet specifies coax cable as its medium.

Ethernet itself implements only the first two layers of the ISO/CCITT model, referring to layers 3–7 as the Client Layer. Hardware/software products from the three developers and from other manufacturers can give you partial implementations of the upper five layers.

One such product is Intel Corporation's iNA 960 network software package. It implements the Transport Layer with Class 4 service. In general, the Data Link Layer's work produces only a "best effort" delivery service. The Transport Layer guarantees reliable message delivery. Developers use iNA 960 software to build systems using the 8086, 8088, and 80186 microprocessors and the 82586 communications co-processor. The

TABLE 6-4
How Some Popular Products Conform to OSI Levels

Level 1	Physical	Ethernet Omninet Transporter
Level 2	Data Link	Ethernet Omninet Transporter
Level 3	Network	Omninet Transporter Xerox Network Systems (XNS) Internet Datagram Protocol Intel Network Architecture (iNA)
Level 4	Transport	Omninet Transporter Corvus Simple Virtual Circuit Xerox Network Systems Intel Network Architecture
Level 5	Session	Constellation II Disk Server Protocol
Level 6	Presentation	Virtual Terminal Protocol Constellation II Name Lookup North American Presentation Layer Protocol Syntax (NAPLPS)

TABLE 6-5
Broadband and Baseband Technology

	BROADBAND	BASEBAND
Transmission	Analog	Digital
Medium	Active	Passive
	CATV cable Fiber optics	Twisted-pair cable Coax cable Fiber optics Microwave
Can the medium fail?	Yes, at headend and other components.	Yes, but only at interface.
Access methods	CSMA/CD	CSMA/CD CSMA/CA CSMA/CP Token-passing Hybrid methods
Muxes	TDM FDM	TDM FDM
Channels	Up to 5	One
Architecture	Branching Tree	Tree, Ring, Bus, Mesh, Double Bus, Hybrids, etc.

82586 or 82501-based hardware implements the Physical and part of the Data Link Layer while the iNA 960 implements the rest of the Data Link Layer as well as Layers 3, 4, and 7.

iNA 960 running on a microprocessor, plus the 82586, would give your system a very efficient communications front end.

Table 6-4 shows how some popular products fit into the OSI model.

Broadband or Baseband?

When you need to make a broadband versus baseband decision, consider the two as complements rather than competitors, designed for different tasks and different needs (Table 6-5). Baseband gives you an inexpensive, simple-to-maintain solution. The more complex, costly broadband technology gives you the advantages of a wider data channel, longer distance travel, and the ability to mix voice and video with data. Broadband finds more sales in large campus-like facilities, either industrial or educational, where long distances separate buildings, or in one multi-story building with need for high-volume data transfer or multiple channels.

You can make your baseband/broadband decision without fear that one or the other will succeed in capturing the entire market; neither technology will disappear in the foreseeable future. In fact, many technology intensive offices have a broadband network and a baseband network, each doing what they do best, connected by a gateway.

THE LOCAL AREA NETWORK DECISION

You bought your microcomputer to improve your productivity. Now you've discovered the advantages that connecting the department's computers can give you. You are ready to make a LAN purchase decision.

Work your way through Table 6-6. This first checklist focuses on your needs.

Question 3 determines whether you need an intelligent interface. The

TABLE 6-6
Your Service Needs

1. Do you need gateways?

2. Do you use or expect to use microcomputers from different manufacturers?

3. Will you be connecting sophisticated 16- and 32-bit microcomputers with ¼ megabyte of main memory or more?

   Or will you connect 8-bit machines with little memory?

4. Do you have a large database that computers attached to the network need to access very heavily (almost constantly)?

5. Most LANs are purchased for use in one work area. Is this your need? (A)

   Or do you need a network spanning many rooms in a small building? (B)

   Or a multi-floor office building? (C)

   Or a multi-building industrial or academic complex? (D)

6. Will you transmit voice and video (as in teleconferencing) as well as data?

computers with substantial amounts of main memory can usually afford the overhead necessary to do what an intelligent interface could do for them. Less powerful computers need an intelligent interface. The trend in networking is toward having the network provide as much service as possible through intelligent interfaces and servers rather than burdening the computer with these tasks. Memory used for network overhead is memory that you can't use for useful application tasks.

If you answered yes to question 4, your network needs a database server. At the least, you should consider a disk server. If you answered yes to question 6, you need a broadband network with an intelligent interface or a fiber optics-based network. The newest fiber optic cables will allow you to put voice and video on individual fibers of a multiple-fiber cable.

Question 5 asks you about the size of the network you need. Choices A and B can use twisted-wire pair or baseband coax cable. You don't need a broadband network unless you also answered yes to question 6, or you really need uniformly high data transfer rates. Choices B, C, and D should investigate fiber optics. Choice C could use a broadband cable running vertically from floor to floor with baseband networks covering each individual floor. Gateways would connect each floor's network to the vertical broadband network. If you chose D, microwave connections between buildings will probably be cost-effective compared to underground coax cables subject to rodent and moisture damage. Be sure to check the alignment of your microwave antennas following a strong earthquake.

Now we'll consider the manufacturers' offerings, beginning with closed and open systems.

An open system accommodates equipment from different manufacturers (Question 2 in Table 6-6). Omninet and Ethernet are examples. A closed system allows only a particular manufacturer's equipment to access the network. Wangnet is a closed network system.

The ISO and CCITT, in creating and endorsing the Open Systems Interconnection Model, have voted in favor of open systems. If you expect that you will purchase all of your network equipment from one manufacturer, you may choose a closed LAN. However, even the closed LAN manufacturers, since open connection will be the ultimate winner of the market, are making plans to allow some amount of open connection as time goes on.

Refer back to Table 6-5 now. Did you choose broadband only? You can move ahead to the next paragraph. Did you choose baseband or a baseband/broadband combination? For the combination, be sure that both manufacturers have working gateways. Now turn back to Table 6-3 and see what your two top medium choices are. Also note if any medium is absolutely precluded from consideration.

Now look at Table 6-1, which covers access methods. Does any access method offer you more advantages than the others?

The cost ingredient in your LAN decision has two parts: initial costs, and maintenance and expansion costs. Don't let a low initial price sway you. Make sure that you know what the expansion costs and maintenance costs will be. Put together a 5-year cost analysis.

Now look at the other side of the equation. What will this solution save you? This is not a simple or trivial question. Before you can determine what you can afford to spend, you must understand how much money you actually spend every day in lost productivity. Calculate how much more money you could generate if your employees didn't waste their daily energy and brain power doing by hand what a machine could do. Only then, with both sides of the equation before you, will you be able to make the best cost decision for your company.

Finally, make a list of your choices from the various checklists. This gives you a profile of the products you're looking for.

The two errors you can make with a LAN decision, equally disastrous, fall into the extremes. You can buy more capability than you need, by getting carried away on a particular manufacturer's or technology's bandwagon. Or your can buy too little capability, forgetting that today's decisions should allow for tomorrow's needs as well. Reread this chapter until you can avoid both pitfalls.

FUTURE OF LOCAL AREA NETWORKS

Local area networks have a bright future in manufacturing and the primary production industries. Their brightest future, however, rests in the office of the future.

Office of the Future

While productivity in manufacturing has risen dramatically in the past hundred years, the productivity of the office worker has not shown dramatic improvement. This low office productivity has a simple cause. The modern office worker still works with 19th-century tools! Since they now enjoy very little capital investment per head, compared with manufacturing workers, office workers can expect substantial productivity gains if they get the needed capital investments. The major victories of the productivity battle do not come from saving money with fewer employees, but in making more money for the business with approximately the same number of employees.

Why should the automated office be your ultimate goal?

The office of the future is to today's office as modern agribusiness is to the farm irrigated with an Archimedes screw. Both today's office and the

Archimedes-serviced farm depend too much on sweat and not enough on human brains.

A totally functioning electronic office may be beyond your business' means, but you can implement a partial solution. From a corporate point of view, the LAN takes a first step toward improving office productivity. Add electronic mail to your LAN and you've taken a giant second step to efficiency.

Electronic Mail

The U.S. Postal Service's recently defunct E-COM system let you send a message to a message center. The messages were printed and put into envelopes. This and similar systems, called Generation II electronic mail, use the regular postal system for message delivery. The screen-to-screen systems, called Generation III electronic mail, include Omnimail for Omninet and products from the sales leaders TYMNET and GTE-Telenet.

The most sophisticated version of electronic mail—voice mail—does not require you to type your message. Simply name the receivers, then dictate your message. The system transmits your message by digitizing your analog voice signals. Then the receiver reconstructs your voice. To partially offset its convenience, voice mail uses a great deal of disk storage. (We'll look at voice technology again in Chapter 8.)

In order to send your messages around the country and around the world, you need to connect your LAN to public packet networks, the subject of the next chapter.

7

public
packet
networks

In this chapter, we move one step outward from your microcomputer-based LAN to examine the world of resources beyond your department and company.

The electronic office in Chapter 6 included electronic mail and other message-handling services in the United States and other nations. How do you, with or without a LAN, send messages to other computers around the world, quickly and easily?

Before answering this specific question, let's look at the structure and services of the communications industry itself.

Common carriers provide basic communication and transportation services to the public. Bus companies in the transportation industry and the telephone companies in the communications industry are examples of common carriers. Specialized common carriers provide specialized common carrier services; microwave links or special satellite channels are a common example. Specialized common carriers in the U.S. include MCI and Sprint. Interstate common carriers face regulation by the Federal Communications Commission (FCC), and companies that operate only within the borders of one state are regulated by the state's public utilities commission.

The latest development in this deregulated communications industry is the value-added carrier (VAC). The VAC leases basic communication services from a common carrier and then adds value in the form of extra services and offers the package to consumers. *Public packet networks (PPNs) are an example of the value-added carrier or value-added network (VAN).*

These public packet networks offers a reasonably inexpensive, convenient way to access other public and private networks, databases, and other subscribing microcomputer owners and communications services. Hospitals connect to medical databases, research firms and government agencies connect to financial databases, banks communicate with each other quickly and efficiently, and manufacturers, oil companies, libraries, and universities all use the public packet networks heavily. The PPNs only offer services to their own *subscribers,* called a closed user group.

Most PPNs levy a monthly service charge on their subscribers, as well as charges based on the amount of traffic each subscriber generates. Of course, you can only use the public packet network to communicate with other members of the closed user group. But many of these other "users" are networks—public and private, national and international—and database services. Let's examine the implications of having other networks as subscribing users.

Suppose you are subscriber A and you want to get a Dow Jones report from fellow subscriber B? That's simple, as illustrated in Figure 7-1.

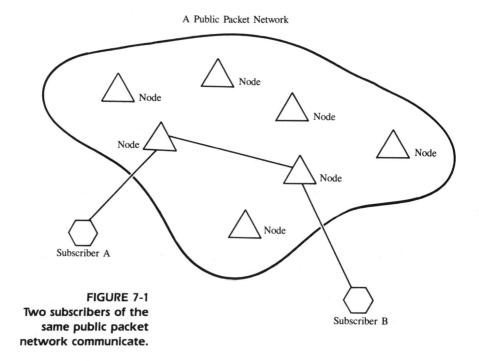

A Public Packet Network

FIGURE 7-1
**Two subscribers of the
same public packet
network communicate.**

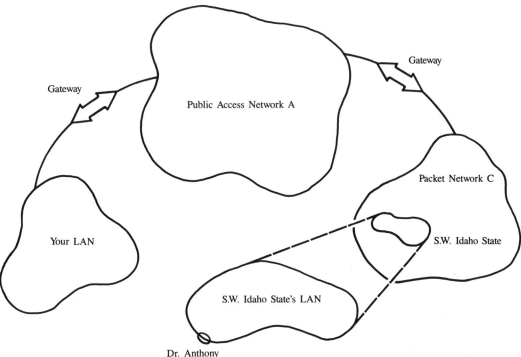

FIGURE 7-2
**A message travels from your LAN to a station
in Northwest Idaho University's LAN, via two
packet networks.**

Now suppose you want to ask Professor S. B. Anthony of the Computer Sciences Department of Northwest Idaho State University a question. You are a member of public packet network A, and Northwest Idaho State isn't. Must you write a letter to Dr. Anthony instead? Not at all. Northwest Idaho State is a subscriber to multi-University packet network C, which is a "user" of your packet network A. Your urgent query travels to network C from network A, and finally arrives at Northwest Idaho State's LAN. Professor Anthony, one station in the LAN, receives her message from the LAN, as shown in Figure 7-2.

When you can communicate with another computer even if more than one gateway stands between the two computers, the subscribers-only restriction has less meaning than it seems to.

There is only one technical requirement you must fulfill before you take advantage of all this communications power. In order to communicate with these value-added carriers, you must use the X.25 interface standard.

OSI

X.25

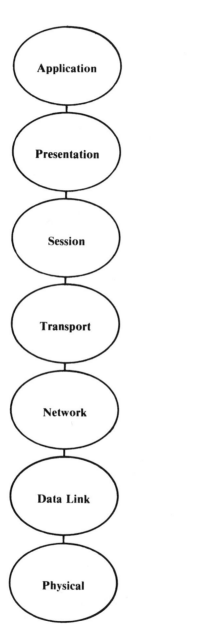
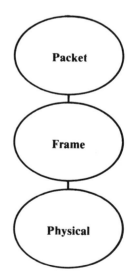

FIGURE 7-3
X.25's three layers and
OSI's equivalents.

X.25

You first encountered X.25 in Chapter 5 as a Network Layer standard. But X.25's real importance lies in its role as a standard for communication with the public packet networks. X.25 is the CCITT's recommended solution for the interface between your computer (a DTE) and the public packet networks.

The X.25 standard for DTE connection to a public packet network covers the first three OSI layers, which it calls the Physical, Frame, and Packet Levels. The Physical Level of X.25 uses the CCITT's X.21 Physical Layer standard, for full-duplex, point-to-point synchronous transmission between your DTE and the public packet network. The Frame Level, corresponding to the OSI's Data Link Layer, controls the actual exchange of data between your DTE and the network, using HDLC (Chapter 4) frames. The Packet Level, OSI's Network Layer, gives the data exchange meaning with packets. X.25 requires Virtual Circuit service at the network layer. Figure 7-3 shows X.25's three layers and OSI's equivalent.

X.25 is a much misunderstood standard, frequently but erroneously treated as though it were an end-to-end protocol. "X.25 networks" are only so called because the DTE connects to the network using the X.25 standard. X.25 has nothing to say about a network's internal operations.

Because a new version of X.25 comes out of the CCITT's Study Group VII (SG VII) every four years, minor differences in X.25 implementations can sometimes cause communications problems. All the study groups that develop the CCITT standards meet for formal adoption meetings every four years. The last such meeting, in 1984, saw new versions of all the X-series standards discussed in this chapter.

The public packet networks in most other countries are agencies of the government's Post, Telegraph and Telephone (PTT) administration. In this situation, you can expect much more uniformity in service within a nation, making intra-country network interconnections much less of a problem. The U.S., without this PTT-imposed uniformity, has more need for standards.

Since the public packet network needs X.25-format packets, your computer must provide X.25-format packets, directly or indirectly. If your computer cannot produce X.25-format packets itself, you must buy or lease a product that will convert your data stream into X.25-format packets.

Table 7-1 summarizes the three options. As your first option, you can write your own X.25 interface software package. If you have a host plus terminals instead of a LAN, you might consider this option beause it gives end-to-end error control (that is, you control the errors all the way from the sending person to the receiving person, not just errors occurring on the transmission path). This first option has the highest cost because of the software development time. The second option—a network vendor-supplied

TABLE 7-1
Three Strategies for X.25 Interfacing

I. Write Your Own X.25 Interface

■ End-to-end error checking

■ Cost of software development

■ Cost of additional equipment

II. Network Vendor-Supplied Lease

■ Easiest solution to implement

■ No end-to-end error control

■ Traffic moves slower than with your own interface

■ Monthly lease cost

(Engine, Mini-Engine and Micro-Engine, discussed later in this chapter, are examples)

III. Certified X.25 PAD Equipment

■ PAD introduces the highest time delay of the three solutions

■ Cost of PAD equipment

■ Can connect many asynchronous devices to a PAD (but so can solution II)

■ No end-to-end error control

lease—is the easiest to implement. We'll discuss this in more detail later in this chapter. The third option is to buy a PAD facility that will packetize your asynchronous data stream.

GTE-Telenet and TYMNET lead the PPN field in the United States. Sixty percent of Telenet's subscribers use options 1 and 3, as does a similar percentage of TYMNET's users. Microcomputers and microcomputer-based LANs form a fast-growing segment of the subscriber base to the packet networks. If your computer is a station in a LAN, the LAN manages your interface to the public packet network, including the X.25 conversion, via a gateway. We'll discuss TYMNET's options for the LAN/TYMNET interface later in this chapter.

Most PPNs have an active certification program, listing the equipment that can produce X.25-format packets ready for transfer on its network.

CCITT PAD STANDARDS

The work of a *packet assembly and disassembly (PAD)* facility depends on three CCITT recommendations. The X.3 standard defines PAD itself: assembly of data into outgoing packets and disassembly of incoming packets into data and control information. The X.28 standard defines the interface between a PAD facility and an asynchronous device, while X.29 defines the interface between the PAD facility and a packet-mode DTE. Most microcomputers produce an asynchronous data stream. Study Group VII, which developed X.25, also developed the X.3, X.28, and X.29 standards. Figure 7-4 illustrates how X.25, X.3, X.28, and X.29 work together.

Some PAD products work only with a particular manufacturer's equipment, while others are generic PAD products.

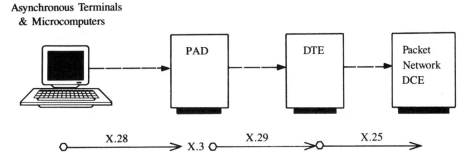

FIGURE 7-4
X.28, X.3, X.29, and X.25 work together to
move asynchronous character data to a public
packet network.

PACKET NETWORK TO PACKET NETWORK

You have the X.25 standard to move packets from your DTE microcomputer to a public packet network. How do you move packets from one public packet network to another, including across international boundaries? The CCITT's X.75 fits the bill, and Figure 7-5 illustrates how.

You now have an interface for your DTE computer to a public packet network and from one packet network to another. But you need much more. How do you communicate with private vendor networks like SNA and DECNET? What do you do when the chain of network connections stretches across five networks from the sender to the ultimate receiver, since X.25 specifies only one DTE/DCE connection?

The CCITT's Study Group VII finally answered this question in 1984 (Figure 7-6), telling system designers to use X.25 for all these interface problems. What does this CCITT decision mean in practical terms? It means that the public net acts as a DTE to the second net's DCE. Using X.25 poses one unified problem for system designers—infinitely preferable to the otherwise impossible job of interfacing idiosyncratic computer message systems.

Consider what happens when two electronic mail systems must pass a message. A message system has a human interface because it is designed to be used by humans and the only entry to the system is by humans. It asks questions and expects responses. When two message systems try to communicate, one system's software must take the place of the human, mimicking

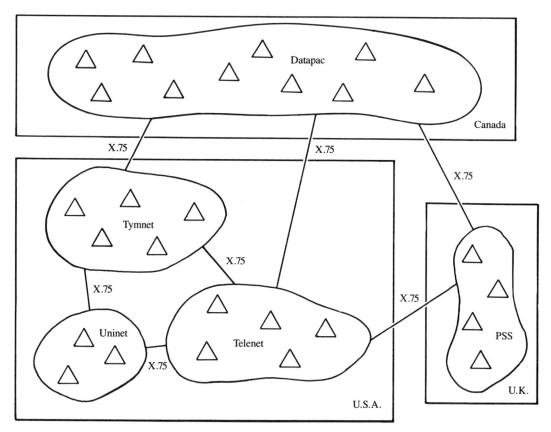

FIGURE 7-5
X.75 connects packet networks.

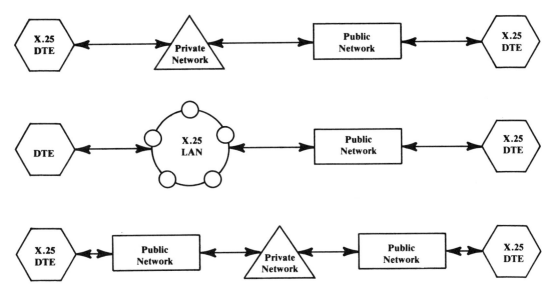

FIGURE 7-6
Three possible configurations the CCITT found a solution for.

human responses—an almost impossibly complex task. If the two systems use X.25, much of this confusion disappears.

Permanent Virtual Circuits

For many applications, you will want one computer or workstation to have contact with only one other destination on the public packet network and you will want these communications to flow as quickly and to be as error-free as possible. For these applications, the Permanent Virtual Circuit (PVC) offers you a quicker connection because the network does not have to assign a Virtual Circuit when it sets up your call; the circuit is permanently assigned. This also gives you an extra security edge because the two sites can communicate only with each other as long as the PVC exists.

The 1980 and 1984 versions of X.25 include the Permanent Virtual Circuit as an optional feature.

USING PUBLIC PACKET NETWORKS

Now you're ready to consider using a public packet network. The two most popular U.S. public packet networks, GTE-Telenet of Vienna, Virginia, and TYMNET of San Jose, California, each have about 40% of the total subscribers in the U.S. and connect easily to Canada's Datapac network. This section of the chapter profiles TYMNET in detail.

In operation since 1971, TYMNET's subscriber base now stands at over 500 with 1300 nodes. But the word "node" does not mean exactly the same thing when TYMNET uses it as it does when a LAN manufacturer uses it.

Nodes

A public packet network is composed of nodes and links between nodes, with each node an intelligent communications processor collecting incoming traffic and routing it toward its destination (Figure 7-9).

There are two kinds of TYMNET nodes: the TYMCOM and the TYM-SAT. TYMCOM nodes work only with hosts. If you want a TYMCOM node on your company's premises, a TYMNET field engineer must install it. If a TYMCOM connects your LAN to TYMNET, the LAN must act like a host.

The TYMSAT node expects asynchronous or synchronous terminal

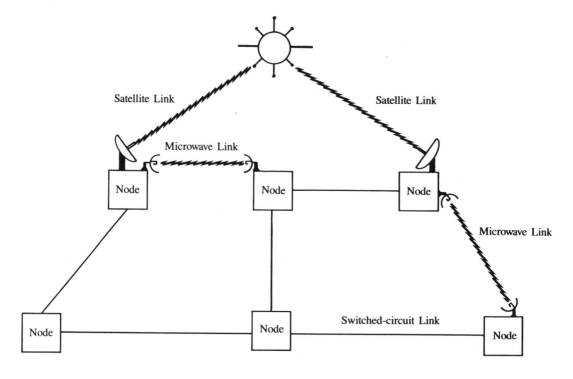

FIGURE-7-7
A public packet network with nodes and circuit-switched, microwave and satellite links.

TABLE 7-2
TYMNET's "Engine" Nodes

	MICRO-ENGINE	MINI-ENGINE	ENGINE
Ports:			
async	16	64	256
sync	8	32	32
Node functions:	Concentrate/Multiplex traffic		
	Network monitoring		
	Protocol, speed, and code conversions		
	Produces a log for accounting		
	Can manage electronic mail		
	Can connect a network gateway to TYMNET		
	Acts as Supervisor		

traffic. Your personal computer can dial into a TYMSAT node and pretend that it's a dumb terminal (a procedure known as emulating a terminal). You can also use a TYMSAT to connect your LAN to TYMNET. The main difference between these two types of nodes is that hosts produce (and TYMCOMs expect) high-speed synchronous traffic while TYMSATs are primarily oriented to low-speed asynchronous traffic.

If you don't want to communicate directly with a TYMCOM or TYMSAT node, TYMNET has three types of nodes that you can buy or lease as intermediaries, either on your own or on TYMNET's premises. The nodes for your premises, called the Engine, Mini-Engine, and Micro-Engine, are full-fledged nodes in the TYMNET network.

Table 7-2 gives you a summary of the capabilities of the Engine, Mini-Engine, and Micro-Engine. (These nodes actually produce packets not in X.25 format, but in TYMNET's internal operations format, called TII.) The three Engines differ mainly in their capacity.

Ports

You can arrange to use TYMNET through either public access ports or private ports. The public ports use either public dialup or WATS (wide area telephone service) facilities, and private ports use either dialup or leased lines. TYMNET has over 10,000 public access ports.

If you choose dialup access to a public port, you must resign yourself to answering a TYMNET node's questions about your identity whenever you want to access the network. Since the public access dialup ports are much more vulnerable to attack by non-subscribers than other access points, every public packet network takes some precautions to keep spies and malicious pranksters out.

You begin by dialing the local TYMNET access number; this connects you to a TYMSAT node. When you hear a high-pitched tone, you have reached the node and can set your modem to transmit and receive data. TYMNET will begin by asking you who you are. In response, it expects a one-letter code from a TYMNET-supplied list. This code tells the node what kind of terminal you're using, so it can send you the right kind of data at the right rate. Most personal computers are "A," corresponding to ASCII at 300 or 1200 bps. Next, TYMNET will ask you to log on. Type in your user name. If you type a name that TYMNET recognizes, it will ask for your password.

Now you're ready to name a receiver and begin communicating. Of course, you can buy software packages that will automate this login procedure. The network automatically sets up a Virtual Circuit for your communication.

If you expect a high-traffic volume, consider a private port. A private port guarantees that your company will never be denied access to the network, regardless of how busy other ports may be, and it means that you can control employee access to the network, since all traffic flows through one port. If you combine a private port with a leased line, you will have the usual higher quality of service and higher costs of leased lines. It also means that you will not have to dial an access number to reach the network. The public packet networks have other special facilities designed for high-traffic customers.

Network Supervision and Control

TYMNET's watchdog program, called Network Supervisor, runs on one of the network's nodes (either a TYMCOM or a TYMSAT), recording, controlling, and supervising network operations. At least four other Supervisors wait on "hot standby," ready to take over immediately if the active Supervisor fails. It's the Supervisor that establishes your bona fides when you log in, creates a Virtual Circuit from sender to receiver, and collects and stores both normal accounting information and error records, among other things.

TYMNET can provide you with this detailed accounting information, including user names, number of characters transmitted during each session, how long each session lasted, and the user names that your station contacted.

TABLE 7-3
Host or Terminal?

1. Do you have a host computer producing high-speed synchronous traffic?

2. Do you have a PBX LAN?

   If you answer yes to question 1 or 2, you produce a host-like traffic pattern. You will have to connect to TYMNET through a TYMCOM node.

3. Do you have a series of asynchronous devices—terminals or microcomputers emulating terminals—not connected into a LAN?

4. Do you have a non-PBX LAN?

   If you answer yes to question 3 or 4, you produce a terminal-like traffic pattern. You will have to connect to TYMNET through a TYMSAT node.

The Service Choice

Given all these choices, how do you decide what's best for your business? First, as always, determine what type of traffic you will generate using Table 7-3.

Then you need to determine the type of TYMNET access you need—in-house or on the road (Table 7-4).

There is still an unanswered question. What do you do if you don't have a host or a LAN, just a single microcomputer? Are you doomed to terminal emulation if you want to tap into the power of the public packet networks?

LANs, Microcomputers, and X.25

The answer is no.

TYMNET's X.PC program—X.25 for a personal computer—solves this problem. X.PC communicates via a TYMSAT with a network server and then to any destination on TYMNET.

With X.PC and similar products, your microcomputer need not hide in a dumb terminal's skin to log on to a PPN's nodes. Up to 15 sessions travel simultaneously over the LAN-to-TYMNET gateway link; you could log on to several databases with the same link, for example.

X.25 for microcomputers is a high priority software development project at many manufacturers because microcomputer users are turning to the

TABLE 7-4
In-House or On The Road?

1. Do you have telecommuting employees, employees who must work from hotel rooms as they travel, or employees who will need dialup access for other reasons?

   You need access to the public dialup ports for at least part of your solution.

2. Do you expect consistently high levels of traffic?

3. Do you need to guarantee your company's access to the packet network?

4. Is your work time critical?

   If you answer yes to question 2, 3, or 4, consider a private port, particularly if you answered "yes" to all three of these questions.

5. Do you prefer to have your TYMNET access point on your premises?

6. Do you need to channel high- and low-speed traffic through one controller?

7. Do you have some host-like traffic and some asynchronous terminal traffic?

   If you answer yes to question 5, 6, or 7, consider an Engine, Mini-Engine or Micro-Engine. If you have a LAN, particularly a LAN with electronic mail, consider an Engine.

PPNs to boost their telecommunications abilities. Some PBX LANs also offer a direct dialin to one or more of the PPNs as one of their services. As the PPNs become more popular, you can expect more and more PBX vendors to design this additional service.

In the next chapter, we'll survey microcomputer applications of voice and videotex technology, the glamor subfields of telecommunications.

8

voice,
video,
text

It's time to turn back to Chapter 6 and reread the description of the office of the future. The office of the future, even more than today's office, communicates. Not surprisingly, most office automation advances involve communications systems, broadly defined. Of all the technologies included in Chapter 6's office of the future, only facsimile (FAX) transmission will not be covered in this book. This chapter focuses on voice technology, and on teletext and videotex services for the office of the present and future.

Let's begin with a look at voice technology.

VOICE

In general, communication can be immediate (as with a telephone call) or delayed (as with a letter). In some cases, nothing but an immediate communication will do. You simply have to pick up your telephone and call.

About 75% of the time, you don't really need immediate communication. Do you have a question? Send a voice or text message and wait for an answer to your question. *Voice mail,* like electronic (text) mail, uses the delayed technique. A computer records, stores, and delivers voice messages, just as it can record, store, and deliver a text message in an electronic mail system.

In fact, why bother with voice mail at all if you can get an electronic mail system for much less cost? Voice mail does have some powerful time-saving inducements. You can talk much faster than you can type. You can talk and do something else: read figures from a report, rummage through the clutter on your desk, or scribble on a calendar. You can emphasize certain words or phrases and, with your inflections, transmit more information than mere words on a screen could. You can easily integrate a voice mail system into your CABX or PABX (described in Chapter 5), since most PABXs have unused capacity. Without a PABX or CABX, you can buy voice mail service through a service bureau and enjoy the time savings of voice versus keyboard input. Voice's great advantage, after speed of composition, lies in its potential for a hands-free environment. We'll discuss the hands-free execution environment later in this chapter.

Delayed messaging by voice mail will help you avoid telephone lag. You send your message and then move on to your next task. Study after study has demonstrated that executives waste too much of their time on the ritual of calling, leaving a message, being called when they are away from their desks, calling back, discovering that the person is in a meeting, and so on. On the average, only 25% of business calls reach the intended receiver on the first try.

Delayed messaging also helps you to lessen the problems involved in doing business across several time zones. If your question or suggestion does not need an immediate answer, a voice message system can prevent the stress of groggy midnight telephoning.

Digitizing Speech

In order to store, transport, and then recreate speech, your computer has to turn the sounds that you make into the digital data that computers handle.

If you multiplex digitized voice traffic with other digital traffic, you use your transmission lines to maximum efficiency (Figure 8-1). Digital data also has the advantage of well-established methods of error control, including forward error correction and data encryption. Finally, digitized speech uses less of the transmission medium because it is much more compact than analog speech on a voice-grade line.

In general, you can *digitize* speech in two ways. The vocoder method depends on banks of hardware filters and works more quickly and precisely than the second method. The vocoder filters divide the signal into frequency ranges. The vocoder analyzes pitch, whether phonemes (the basic unit of

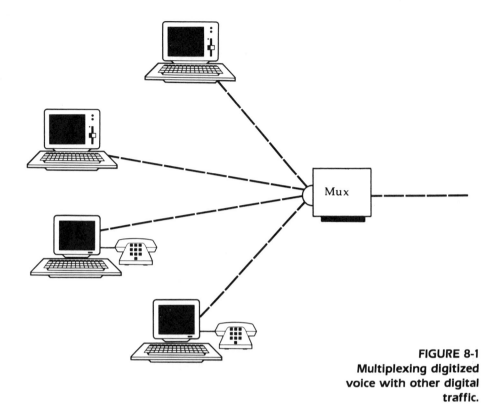

FIGURE 8-1
Multiplexing digitized
voice with other digital
traffic.

spoken language, like the "b" in bat) are voiced or unvoiced, and the parameters of the vocal tract producing the sounds. The larger and more powerful speech digitization systems use vocoder hardware.

The second method of digitization, called waveform analysis, depends on digitization of the analog wave that the speech forms. This analysis depends on software rather than hardware. The software approach requires the use of statistical approximation, particularly Fourier analysis, which slows the process as well as being less precise. Your advantage comes from its lower cost. The commonest form of waveform analysis, called pulse code modulation (PCM), uses a codec. Figure 8-2 illustrates both kinds of voice digitization.

The process of digitization with a waveform analyzer or a vocoder reproduces the low-frequency sounds much more fully and accurately than high-frequency sounds. This explains why a deep voice generally experiences better results than a high-pitched voice.

In a voice mail system, all the computer does is record, store, and then deliver messages. It does not have to understand anything. The next section of this chapter shows how a computer understands your voice commands.

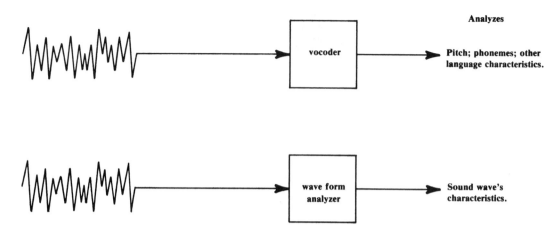

FIGURE 8-2
Speech digitization.

Speech Recognition

Voice recognition has many potential applications. Vending machines could listen to your commands, telephones could connect you to a number based on your speaking the number rather than typing it, you could make verbal database queries, and you could input voice data during an inventory or in any other situation where a hands-free environment improves productivity. Voice applications have their greatest applications where they can replace several keystrokes. In most situations, remember, people make fewer mistakes when reciting numbers than when typing numbers, particularly when they are tired or distracted.

Direct speech transcription—talking to your keyboard to receive a typed report—is strictly science fiction at present and will remain so for the rest of the 1980s at least.

The most interesting existing business application is the voice command-driven executive workstation. Before looking at an actual product, we need an overview of the technology.

Independent or Dependent?

A *speaker-dependent* system expects only one voice. It typically understands more words and has a higher dependability than an independent system. A *speaker-independent* system can respond to any voice—in theory. Because it must do a great deal of statistical analysis, a speaker-indepen-

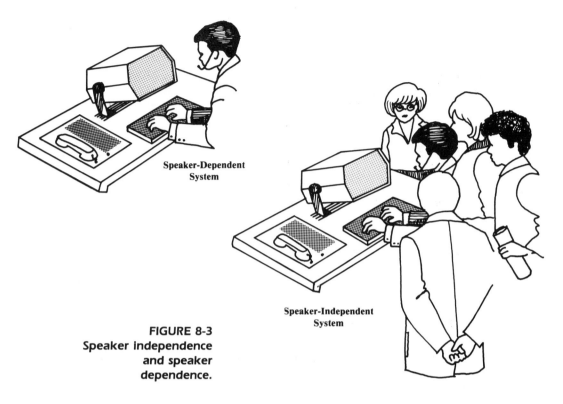

Speaker-Dependent
System

Speaker-Independent
System

FIGURE 8-3
Speaker independence
and speaker
dependence.

dent system requires more memory. Most office systems are speaker-independent so they can be used by more than one person (Figure 8-3).

With either dependence or independence, you must train the computer to understand a list of keywords and commands. Just as you do when you are training a person in a new language, you will pick a word, then pronounce the word several times. The computer will record and analyze your several samples and come up with an average analysis, called a template, or *signature* (see Table 8-1).

Discrete or Continuous?

A word in isolation forms discrete speech. If you say a complete sentence, but separate each word with silence (halt the movement of columns of air for long enough for the computer to recognize that the word has ended), you also have discrete speech. Continuous speech—where one word flows into the next—causes problems for persons trying to learn any new language (Table 8-2). If humans are often baffled, can you imagine the problems that a computer has with continuous speech?

A computer "recognizes" speech by a process of pattern-matching. It

TABLE 8-1
The Process of Training

Although systems differ in specifics, this is how you train your voice system to understand the command "Print the file."

1. Type "Print" or point to the word on a list.

2. Say "Print." Speak clearly but naturally. Be sure that you train your system in the same sort of environment that you will use the system in—either quiet office or noisy Stock Exchange floor.

3. Repeat "Print" two to four more times.

4. Move to the word "file" and repeat steps 2 and 3 with "file."

5. Switch from training mode to command mode.

6. Choose a file for printing. Display its contents on your computer's screen.

7. Say "Print the file <pause>." or "Print file <pause>."

8. The computer understands "print" and "file." The contents of the file displayed on your screen begin to print.

compares its analysis of what you are currently saying with the collection of templates it has on file. A single word has a clear beginning and end. This kind of pattern-matching works smoothly.

With an unbroken signature that may contain several words, your computer must decide when the sound level has dropped low enough to justify calling a word break. It will scan the signature, looking for a match

TABLE 8-2
Discrete and Continuous Speech

DISCRETE SPEECH	CONTINUOUS SPEECH
<p> Seven <p>	<p> Give me a pie chart of the export figures and when you're done, send the file to the printer. <p>
<p> Twenty-nine <p>	
<p> Print <p>	
<p> File <p>	
<p> Print <p> file <p>	
<p> Print <p> the <p> file <p>	<p> Print the file. <p>
<p> Graph <p>	

<p> means a 10–30 millisecond pause.

between what it sees and its library of words. What happens if a word has a naturally occurring pause in it? What about the letters that don't produce strong, distinct air movements? Your speech-recognition system may very well create "words" that conform to no known human language.

Challenges in Speech Recognition

Your computer recognizes significant words through a process of pattern-matching. Needless to say, it will never find an exact match. The question comes down to: how close is close enough?

This is not an idle question. All the computer sees is the movement of air, and that's all that speech means to it. To a vocoder or waveform analyzer, the letter "s" looks a great deal like the letter "t"; "t" looks a great deal like "p"; and "c" looks like "e." That explains why voice recognition systems can fail to understand the difference between "start" and "stop." If you are a disabled person depending on a voice-activated wheelchair, your system must be able to distinguish these crucial words dependably.

Voice recognition systems may also have trouble when one word is embedded in another word, as "six" is in "sixteen." Number recognition is particularly important in business applications, of course.

Pitch shifts create another set of problems. A word will have a different pitch depending on the sex of the speaker (less of a problem with waveform analyzers than with vocoders) or on how a word is stressed in the sentence. For example, your computer sees a very different pattern in these two sentences:

She wants to go to Massachusetts?

or

She wants to go to *Massachusetts?*

If you ask the computer:

Don't you recognize *James* Rittenhouse?

the answer will probably be no, even if the computer has a signature for James Rittenhouse stored. The stress gave the word a different signature.

With continuous speech, you have a problem with speed shifts that discrete speech avoids. When words flow together, the speed at which you talk affects how you push the air around and this changes what your computer sees.

Finally, every language has regional accents. If your system must accommodate people from Vermont and South Carolina or Illinois and Hawaii, it will need more processing power and on-board memory than a system whose users all were born and raised in Nashville, Tennessee.

TABLE 8-3
A Hands-Free Executive Workstation

- *Answers your telephone and records messages from callers.*

- *Allows you to call your office and listen to your messages.*

- *Transmits pre-recorded messages at whatever time you set.*

- *Transmits the same message to a whole series of numbers you select.*

- *Stores telephone numbers.*

- *Lets you "dial" a telephone number by saying the numbers rather than pressing buttons.*

- *Records dictation: memos, reports, letters.*

- *Lets you annotate rough drafts with voice comments that guide your administrative assistant in making final revisions.*

- *Lets you annotate a memo that asked for comments. Just make your verbal comments and indicate where your comments should be inserted.*

- *Reminds you of appointments with its calendar.*

- *Alarm rings at pre-set times.*

- *Receives voice mail messages.*

The Hands-Free Executive Workstation

Several companies, impressed with the potential of a hands-free executive work environment, have produced products to create this environment. One such product is the Texas Instruments Speech Command System, designed for the MS-DOS operating system and the TI Professional computer.

The Speech Command System gives you the equivalent of an answering machine, dictation machine, auto-dial telephone, calendar, voice mail system, and daily activities log. The auto-dial phone can hold up to 150 telephone numbers. With the voice mail system, you can record a message and then send it to a list of telephone numbers. You can record a message and set it to transmit at some specific time later in the day—even if you are out of your office at that time.

You train your system to understand important words and commands, like "file" and "graph." Then you can give commands using these words in a sentence. This means that you can say "Graph the file," and the system will respond to "Graph" and "file."

The hands-free executive workstation (Table 8-3), of which this Texas Instruments product is one example, aims to move as many functions as possible into one compact "box," clearing your desk of the otherwise necessary jumble of different machines.

ISDN and the Office of the Future

Since voice can be digitized, the benefits of voice/data integration shown in Figure 8-1 will inevitably come to the office. At present, voice/data integration is mostly an interesting potential rather than an easily installable reality.

The Bell System's Integrated Services Digital Network (ISDN) idea has strong industry support for a future integrated voice/data method, with different versions for residential and large and small business needs. ISDN places telephone, videotex, and ordinary data into one stream, using one medium very efficiently.

Study Group XVII (SG XVII) of the CCITT has been developing a standard for integrated voice and data, but no international standard was proposed at the 1984 CCITT meetings. SG XVII seems to be considering digital PBXs as the most logical base for an integrated office solution.

TELETEXT AND VIDEOTEX

Videotex can be defined as an interactive text and graphics service, bringing you pages of text and graphics that you can collect information from, make purchases and other decisions from, or be entertained with. You can receive the videotex service on a special videotex terminal, on your television set with a special decoder, over a cable TV channel, or over telephone lines to your modem-equipped computer. Videotex does not belong to a particular medium, and it certainly isn't a medium itself (Figure 8-4).

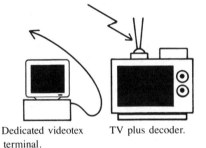

Dedicated videotex terminal.   TV plus decoder.

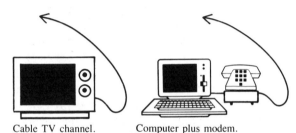

Cable TV channel.   Computer plus modem.

FIGURE 8-4
Videotex and teletext services for the office.

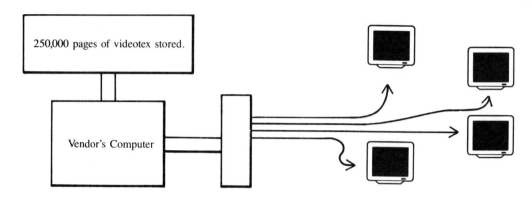

FIGURE 8-5
IPs provide pages.

If your text and graphics service does not allow you to answer or make decisions, you have *teletext*. Since it isn't interactive, teletext uses broadcast media almost exclusively: the unused portion of the commercial TV signal plus a decoder; part of an FM broadcast signal plus a decoder; or a cable TV channel.

A videotex vendor contracts with information providers (IPs) who contribute *pages* to the vendor's total offering (Figure 8-5). The pages form a database that exists on the vendor's computer, usually a mainframe.

The subscribers typically work with a series of menus to locate the precise service they want and pay monthly charges based on the number of pages they view.

Most videotex IPs provide either information retrieval or transaction services. The transaction providers allow you to purchase travel services, clothing, automobiles, and other items, and transact business with your bank. Banks have been particularly interested in providing videotex services to their customers because of the growing costs of paper-based transactions. News, weather reports, stock prices, and database queries all come under the information retrieval heading. A smaller number of IPs provide entertainment—particularly games, puzzles, and jokes. Teletext IPs include everything except the interactive transactions. Table 8-4 shows typical videotex and teletext services.

Videotex was born in Great Britain in 1979 when the Prestel system went into commercial service. Subscribers use either special videotex terminals or a decoder that attaches to a TV set. These methods provide a relatively low-cost way to reach home users, but few businesses seem interested in adding special videotex terminals or decoder-equipped TV sets to the already overcrowded executive desk.

The typical U.S. office seems interested in videotex services accessible

TABLE 8-4
Typical Videotex and Teletext Services

Both videotex and teletext offer these:
  News summaries from selected newspapers
  Sports news and statistics
  Weather reports, local and non-local
  Stock market reports from selected exchanges
  Recent performance of a selected stock
  Financial newsletters
  Joke of the day
  Travel agent listings, available tours, cruises, schedules, prices, etc.

Only videotex offers these:
  Request balance for a specific account at your bank
  Transfer funds from one account to another
  Pay a bank's credit card bill
  Purchase merchandise from an electronic catalog
  Database queries, including specific financial analyses
  Purchase of travel arrangements
  Interactive games

through a microcomputer or LAN. To some extent, this microcomputers versus decoders and dedicated terminals dichotomy has shaped the way the U.S. and European videotex vendors view their markets. This dichotomy has also led directly to a standards battle.

The Great Standards Battle

In Table 6-4, *NAPLPS* appeared as a Presentation Layer protocol. In fact, the North American Presentation Layer Protocol Syntax forms a de facto videotex standard for the United States and Canada, supported by the Canadian Standards Association (CSA) in Canada and ANSI in the United States.

The Comité European des Postes et Telephones (CEPT), an association composed of European PTTs, developed its own videotex standard in 1981, based upon Prestel.

The disarray in the videotex world is reflected in the teletext world as well. The North American teletext standard, called the North American Broadcast Teletext Specification (NABTS), does not resemble the CEPT teletext standard.

NAPLPS uses a virtual coordinate system to define points when creating graphics. This means that NAPLPS ignores the details of the hardware it runs on, depending on an underlying software layer to deal directly with the specific hardware. Untied to any particular manufacturer, NAPLPS aims to run on all popular brands of microcomputers.

This standards battle stems in part from two different perceptions of the audience and its needs. NAPLPS expects the future of videotex to include large numbers of microcomputers, in the home and in the office. The Prestel-inspired CEPT specification is more oriented to special videotex terminals.

Another NAPLPS/CEPT difference centers on the question of how much a user should have to spend on the graphics. The North American consensus seems to be that without NAPLPS-quality graphics, advertisers won't be able to adequately represent products and entice customers to buy. Of course, the higher quality graphics require more processing power and processing power must be paid for. The CEPT strategy has been to emphasize low cost.

Continent-wide standards are better than no standards at all, of course, but one international standard would be even better.

International Videotex

Many nations are developing videotex services as part of their nation's PTT service.

France's national videotex service, called Teletel, is part of a vigorous national videotex effort. Teletel links to a national electronic telephone directory service, which the French government expects to cover the entire country by 1988. With 20 million terminals and no printed directories, the government expects to save millions of francs every year.

The Netherlands' Viditel and the Federal Republic of Germany's Bildschirmtext both follow the CEPT standard. Based on preliminary trials of the Bildschirmtext system, most subscribers come from the business and financial communities.

In Japan, the CAPTAIN (Character and Pattern Telephone Access Information Network) system grew from an early collaboration between the Ministry of Posts and Telecommunications (the Japanese PTT) and the Nippon Telephone and Telegraph Company (NTT). CAPTAIN uses individual addressing of every point on the screen (bit-mapped grahics) instead of the techniques other services use for lower-quality graphics. Bit-mapping uses a great deal more memory and introduces delays. However, CAPTAIN must accept these disadvantages because it cannot use the simple character sets other languages use.

CAPTAIN must cope with three different kinds of writing. Kanji is the

Japanese language expressed in ideographs. Each of the tens of thousands of words must be drawn by the videotex service using its bit-mapping. Kantakana and Hirakana express Japanese through the Latin alphabet, using printing and cursive writing respectively.

The Canadian Telidon system earns praise for its high-quality, sophisticated graphics, an important plus for information providers who are advertisers and sellers of a product. Telidon's high costs stem from its high-quality graphics.

Of course, none of these services claims exclusive jurisdiction in its home country. Telidon offers videotex services in Japan, and both Telidon and Prestel have respectably sized subscriber bases in the United States, for example. Prestel service, as offered in the U.S., is based on a microcomputer network rather than a mainframe.

Other nations are experimenting with videotex and teletext, with the backing of their respective PTTs. Only the United States lacks a single unified videotex offering because of the lack of strong government involvement.

Public Policy Issues

The public policy issues associated with videotex and to a lesser extent teletext resolve themselves into three major categories:

1. Who is allowed to be an IP? Who has access to this information channel?

2. Does anything except the marketplace control content?

3. Does anyone control what the service providers do with the data they collect on specific subscribers' buying habits?

The first question concerns the ability of all purveyors of information to get their chance to reach the American people. If capacity is infinite, all IPs can be accommodated. What if capacity is not infinite? Does the service provider have the right to decide what services will be provided? Can a videotex vendor refuse to deal with a specific IP because of the race, sex, marital status, or political affiliations of the specific IP's owners?

The second question resolves itself into questions about pornography, false advertising, and other legal issues. For example, if an IP is guilty of false advertising or fraud, is the videotex vendor liable for damages as well as the guilty IP? Who decides what constitutes pornography? Home viewers seem more concerned with this issue than business users.

The third question involves privacy issues. Videotex vendors routinely collect information on each subscriber, including specific pages viewed, purchases made, and so on. What use will vendors make of this information? Will they sell names, addresses, and telephone numbers with complete profiles of personal habits and preferences to the highest bidder? Even selling a list of subscribers who chose pages on a specific subject constitutes a massive invasion of subscriber privacy.

The U.S. and state governments are considering laws to protect the privacy of videotex subscribers. User fears on these issues may also be slowing acceptance of videotex, particularly in the home market. The videotex industry, hoping to police itself, announced a series of privacy guidelines developed by the Videotex Industry Association in 1983. Under these guidelines, no information about subscribers can be disclosed without the subscriber's written permission or a court order.

Prospects for Videotex in the U.S.

In 1984, IBM, CBS, and Sears, Roebuck and Company announced plans to offer a videotex product, called Trintex, sometime after 1986. Aimed at home users, this service will provide all the services that have proved successsful in smaller scale services and trials: home banking, interactive shopping, movie and restaurant guides, and games. The participants described themselves as an expert in development and marketing of information and entertainment (CBS), an expert in computer technology (IBM), and an expert in retail marketing (Sears). Trintex expects to market its service to subscribers using any of the popular home computers.

The IPs for this service won't be ignoring the business customers in their rush for the more lucrative home market. News services, stock market reports, investment services, and other typical business services will attract many IPs.

This venture may attract many more users to videotex. Although the market has grown steadily through the early and mid-1980s, growth has not been as explosive as the industry had hoped and predicted. Lack of a single videotex standard seems to be one reason.

Another more fundamental reason may be the fact that no one—either in business or in the home—is used to paying for information. Inexpensive newspapers, free libraries, and free information and entertainment on commercial and non-commercial television channels have convinced Americans that information has no monetary value. But information has never really been free. Libraries are publicly supported, commercial television earns revenue from advertisers, and non-commercial stations receive support from donations and government grants. This information is paid for, albeit indirectly.

It was a shock to business and home consumers when a new class of information providers required direct payment for information. But business is starting to examine the role of information in its life and the value of quick, efficient access to information.

Both teletext and videotex may eventually find their major market in the home. Certainly, the vendors hope so since the home market outnumbers and outspends the business market. Until the end of the 1980s, though, teletext and videotex will remain heavily influenced by what business needs and wants.

What business seems to need is a microcomputer-based integrated information system, including LAN, VAN, and videotex services. Most businesses will wait until the end of the 1980s to find this desire turned into reality.

9

security

A man walks into the communications room where bank employees transfer funds from bank to bank. Using one of the telephones, he calls the funds transfer department of a large bank in Los Angeles and asks for a transfer of $10.2 million dollars to a Swiss bank. When he stumbles over one of the authorization codes, the helpful clerk coaches him through his "memory lapse." The man then uses the bank phone to call the Swiss bank. They transfer the $10.2 million dollars to his bank account.

Fiction? No. The year was 1978. The bank never discovered the multi-million dollar theft. The man talked to his attorney, who called the FBI.

The stakes certainly are high in the banking world. The U.S. Treasury Department disburses checks whose value tops $910 billion every year. The Federal Reserve System, custodian of the nation's financial security, is another prime target, as are the "banker's banks," the banks that deal only with other banks, handling funds transfers in the millions of dollars at the touch of a button.

The security question plagues more than just banks. The estimated cost of security lapses runs from a minimum of $350 million a year to $2 billion.

Back in the days when "computer" meant mainframe and the computer's lair was a remote, temperature-controlled computer center, security was the data processing department's responsibility. Now that computing is both decentralized and ubiquitous with quick and easy data access, potential spies and saboteurs find much easier pickings.

Yet most businesses downplay security issues. Fearing loss of business and hoping that ignoring the dangers will hold them at bay, they fail to develop a security policy.

This chapter will help you to develop a healthy security consciousness.

SOURCES OF DANGER

First, who do you have to fear?

Your own and foreign governments have the ability to spy on your operations. Industrial spies—your competitors—have even more interest in the details of your business. Organized crime has much to win from your corporate information. Your employees can subvert security from within. And finally, individuals will try to get into your computer system for malicious mischief or as a prank. All these people pose a danger to you; only the degree of danger differs.

Next, what attacks will these people use?

If your system includes dialup access, your major danger comes from the public dialup ports.

Public Dialup Ports

Anyone with a microcomputer and a modem with an automatic dialer can program the computer to dial numbers randomly until it reaches the high-pitched tone of another computer's modem.

At the very least you should require a valid user name and password from anyone attempting a logon through the public access ports. Passwords, the most widely used form of protection, usually form a first line of defense for a system. The best protection comes if your company distributes passwords to employees, changing them at least once a month. Research indicates that employee-chosen passwords are almost always laughably easy to guess. Names of the spouse, child, favorite pet, or sports team head the list of obvious passwords. If you allow employees to choose their own passwords, insist that they not pick a word from any of these obvious categories. Make sure that your system uses long passwords and insist that your employees create passwords that stretch to their full allowable length. It will take a thief longer to guess a 10-character password than a 2-character password.

In place of or in addition to the password, you can purchase software that responds only to special tones. Without the device that produces the tone, an intruder cannot log on.

TABLE 9-1
Security for Your Public Dialup Ports

■ Require valid user name.

■ Require valid, unique password.

    a. It must be long.

    b. It should be company-chosen or imaginative.

    c. It must be secret.

■ Require devices that give the dialup port a special tone.

■ Use call-back to authorized location only.

The most effective protection scheme, called *call-back,* has a list of authorized dialup users, their passwords, and the locations they will log on from. The system asks for the user name and password and if they are correct, the system breaks the connection and calls the employee at the authorized phone number (Table 9-1). A joy-riding intruder cannot get access to your system this way and neither can an employee calling in from home or another unauthorized location.

This blocks intruders before they get in. But what happens when the intruder is already in?

Attacks From Within

Your employees, acting from greed, malice, or carelessness, can cause losses through the public access ports, but there are other security precautions you can take in-house.

As a first step, even if you take no other security precautions, you should develop and publicize a security policy and procedures. If you don't have a publicized procedure stating what employees should and should not do (even if it seems self-evident to you), you may not be able to prosecute or otherwise punish an employee who damages or compromises security.

After your security policies are posted and publicized, you can consider the next step. To secure the computer itself, you can install a card/key lock, requiring the user to have a card or key to use the computer system or network station. Then give a card or key only to those employees who should have access to the system.

We discussed passwords in the previous section. In addition to ensuring that employees choose passwords that will challenge the ingenuity of intruders, you must prepare to ensure that employees do not abuse security in departments other than their own. Insisting that employees never divulge a password without permission from their manager will help to prevent this.

Pay close attention to which individuals have system management powers. Who needs to have authority to create new files? Almost everyone. But what about creating new volumes? Who should be able to change their own access to volumes? To control other users? Particularly if you choose to create a local area network, the advantage of decentralized processing should not blind you to the need for a hierarchy of access. With Omninet, for example, you can give every station System Manager status. You can also reserve some powers to particular individuals (certain user names, to be precise). Most LANs give you this choice. Make it carefully.

Every file in your system should protect itself from unauthorized access as well. Every file that is not open to every employee of the company should have a list of persons approved for access to it. Any user not privileged to see the file should be denied access to it—and the attempt should be logged so the attempted breach of security doesn't succeed next time. Ask your local area network vendor about file security before you make a purchase decision. Table 9-2 summarizes suggested in-house security policies.

It's time to consider security issues in the LAN.

TABLE 9-2
Security Policies for Your Employees

■ Post and publicize security dos and don'ts.

■ Use cards or keys to lock hardware.

■ Use secret, unique, imaginative passwords.

■ Prevent passing passwords between employees without manager approval.

■ Regulate who has access to System Manager powers.

■ Help the file system to protect itself.

Weak Points in a Local Area Network

When you consider your network's security, try to think of your system as a load-bearing structure. Your network has its weak points at its joints, the places where components come together. Every connection between your network and the outside world is a potential entry point for spies and

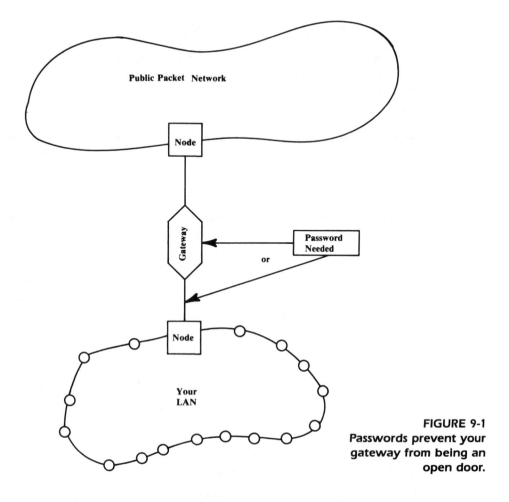

FIGURE 9-1
Passwords prevent your gateway from being an open door.

saboteurs. The third weak point in your system's security comes from your gateways and other connections.

A gateway is a door. Like any other door, it allows two-way traffic. Your job is to ensure that any traffic into your LAN from the outside is traffic that you welcome. The most straightforward way to accomplish this is to require all incoming traffic to authenticate itself (Figure 9-1).

One form of LAN security is available only to broadband. If you have different departments on different channels and you don't implement bridges between the channels, employees from one department cannot reach data belonging to another department (Figure 9-2). Although communication between departments increases the power of your network in general, you might consider isolating the Payroll/Employee Records function on its own channel, for example.

On the plus side, your packet-based LAN already gives you more protection than a message transfer system would because a packet only contains part of a message. An intercepted packet gives much less information than an intercepted complete message.

Electronic Mail

Electronic mail on your LAN is as secure or insecure as your network as a whole. Electronic mail on a public packet network (PPN) is as secure or insecure as the PPN itself.

If you decide to purchase an electronic mail system without a LAN, the mail system will reside on a mainframe owned by the mail system's vendor. You should ask the vendor about the mainframe's security before entrusting your company's communications to the system. Specifically, ask if a break-in at another customer's site or through another customer's dialup ports will give the intruder access to every other customer's files. The answer is almost always "yes." If you will have to add your own security software to protect your company's communications, you must add the cost of this additional software to obtain the total cost of the electronic mail system. You should also investigate the ability of another customer to get access to your files. If the electronic mail vendor services your major competitors and does not provide strong security, you have a particular reason for concern.

The best security for the senders and receivers in an electronic mail system comes from *digital signatures,* appended to the end of or an integral part of the message. These bits are called signatures because they serve the same purpose as the final signature in a paper letter—they show who sent the letter. But a digital signature does better than that! A digital signature ensures four things: no one has forged the sender's signature (digital signatures are unforgeable); the sender cannot deny that the message was

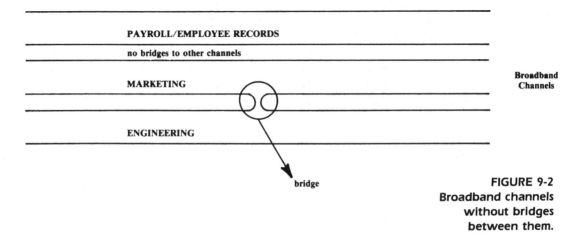

FIGURE 9-2
Broadband channels
without bridges
between them.

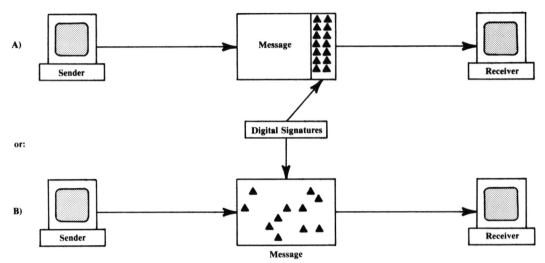

FIGURE 9-3
Digital signatures.

sent; no one tampered with the message en route; the receiver did not tamper with the message. Any tampering with the message, before or after arrival at the receiver's station, changes the digital signature. In order to be able to accomplish all four security features, every message has a unique digital signature (Figure 9-3).

When GTE-Telenet's Telemail electronic mail system was broken into, it sparked a lot of interest in the security of electronic mail systems and the legal status of electronic mail. Some of the conclusions are disquieting.

One of the great advantages of electronic mail systems—detailed, centralized records—also gives it its great weakness. Any person or agency that gains access to the system can collect detailed, centralized records and efficiently invade these private communications.

This situation becomes particularly disquieting when one realizes from the consensus of legal experts that electronic mail does not enjoy the same absolute protection, under U.S. law, that First Class mail does. Without a search warrant signed by a Federal judge, any infringement of First Class mail by any party constitutes a felony. Infringement of electronic mail apparently carries only misdemeanor penalties.

Data Concealment En Route

Another source of danger comes from assaults on the medium itself, in the form of taps. Taps of twisted-pair and coaxial cable are as easy as they are undetectable.

TABLE 9-3
Substitution and Transposition Ciphers

Substitution Cipher

Turns plaintext into ciphertext by beginning the alphabet with a letter other than A. For example:

NORMAL	SUBSTITUTE
a	s
b	t
c	u
d	v
e	w
f	x
g	y
h	z
i	a
j	b

With this cipher, ciphertext "vwuc" stands for cleartext "deck."

Transportation Cipher

Pick a word or phrase that does not contain the same letter more than once. Write it down, then number each letter in the order it appears in the alphabet. Create columns. Now write your cleartext, with one letter per column. The ciphertext is

the contents of Column 1, followed by the contents of Columns 2–7 in numerical order.

This example shows a hypothetical message from Brig. Gen. Francis "Swamp Fox" Marion to Brig. Gen. Daniel Morgan just before Morgan beat Lt. Colonel Banastre Tarleton at Cowpens.

Morgan read:

TNNMEHTYNISRAEGTNWEAOSTTENT
ICTIRSVTCOFAASLPLOOOGSEERLE
FAEDMMAATNOOOAWTSHIDHGMBRLE
JVRSUFPNEI

Which told him:

Tarleton's Legion left camp Jan. 12 with orders to smash you. Moving fast. Dispatch sent to [Major General Nathaniel] Greene. F. Marion

```
COWPENS
1475236

TARLETO
NSLEGIO
NLEFTCA
MPJANTW
ELVEWIT
HORDERS
TOSMASH
YOUMOVI
NGFASTD
ISPATCH
SENTTOG
REENEFM
ARIONAB
```

In addition to preventing taps to your system, you can camouflage the data while they travel on the medium. If your packets are transmitted through a microwave link with the medium not confined to your premises and under your control, you have a particular need to protect the data en route. Satellite broadcasts to your LAN or from your LAN are other candidates for camouflage.

You first learned to camouflage data in your childhood. Do you remember sending "secret" messages to your playground friends in which you substituted one letter for another? Known as substitution and transposition *ciphers,* these kinds of concealment are very easy to crack (Table 9-3).

All schemes for data concealment can be cracked given a large enough sample of the data. For real safety, you cannot conceal the data. You must scramble the data so that no receiver can unscramble it except the intended receiver. Data encryption is the most complex form of data scrambling. Your unscrambled text—*cleartext*—becomes *ciphertext* when it passes through a key. Ciphertext, also called encrypted text, becomes cleartext when it is decrypted by a receiver who has the same key. The *key* "acts" on the cleartext to product ciphertext (Figure 9-4).

You cannot infer or derive the key from an analysis on the ciphertext without expending a great deal of effort. This gives the key method its great power.

In 1977, the National Bureau of Standards published a Data Encryption Standard (DES). This U.S. standard calls for a 56-bit key for encrypting the data and 8 bits for a parity check, giving a total of 64 bits for the key. DES

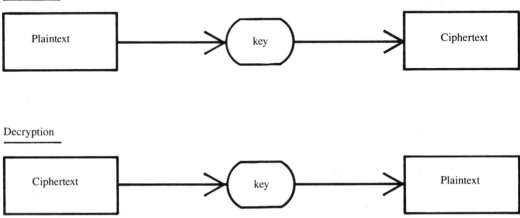

FIGURE 9-4
A key acts on cleartext
to product ciphertext.

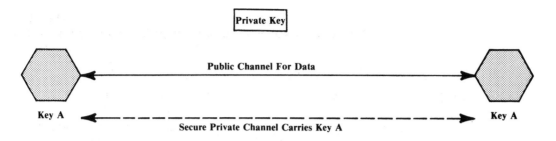

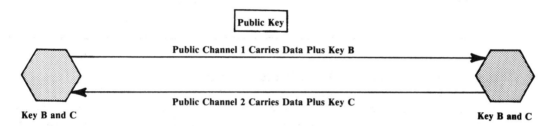

FIGURE 9-5
Private and public keys.

transforms 64 bits of cleartext into 64 bits of ciphertext by passing it through this 56-bit key.

With the DES type of key, called a private key, both sender and receiver use the same key. Because the key is sent over a secure channel before the session starts, the encrypted data can travel safely over the inexpensive public channels. In the public key system, both sender and receiver have two keys. Each side keeps one key secret and transmits the other one. Each decrypts using the secret key. Neither the public nor the private key option has an intrinsic superiority, although manufacturers of the two types of keys engage in a lively debate on the subject (Figure 9.5).

We discussed the Sytek LocalNet LAN in Chapter 6. The LocalNet PCU-20 has an option for a Secure Packet Communication Unit (SPCU) with DES-standard end-to-end encryption. You can choose either encrypted or unencrypted mode for each session. Just as with any other form of private key encryption, the SPCU asks the Key Distribution Center for a key just before the start of a session and the key travels on a secure channel.

Encryption is a Presentation Layer process. However, this refers only to where the work occurs logically. You can actually do the work of encryption

TABLE 9-4
Data Link Layer Encryption versus End-to-End Encryption

DLE	EE
Encrypts the entire packet.	The Data Link Header isn't encrypted.
Data Link Layer management chooses the encryption details.	User chooses encryption details, particularly at Application Layer.
Encrypts at Data Link Layer.	Encrypts at Application or Presentation Layer.
Masks the traffic characteristics.	Does not mask the traffic characteristics.
Not suitable for LANs.	Highest layer encryption gives maximum security.

at any of the layers. Data Link Encryption (DLE) occurs at the Data Link Layer while End-to-End Encryption (EE) occurs at the Presentation or Application Layer. Table 9-4 summarizes the pros and cons of both choices.

Every advantage carries a cost, of course. Data encryption frequently slows system response time.

SECURITY IN PUBLIC PACKET NETWORKS

The public packet networks divide into two camps on the security issue. Datapac and TYMNET believe that the network has a responsibility to enforce strong security measures. GTE-Telenet believes that the security decision properly belongs to the individual subscribers. It implements fewer security measures, preferring a more "friendly" user interface. Most information in this section refers to TYMNET, the PPN profiled in Chapter 7.

The place to start, of course, is with passwords. TYMNET gives you the freedom to choose your own user names and passwords, which is dangerous because it puts the responsibility for password protection squarely on your company's shoulders. It also means that you will have to take pains to ensure that your employees don't choose the easily guessed passwords that we discussed earlier in this chapter. A system of PPN-provided passwords that change frequently provides much more powerful security.

For extra security, TYMNET moves your password in one direction only. Once you enter your password, only the Network Supervisor can read it back.

TYMNET also uses source/destination filtering. A particular user name and password can only log on to a particular node in a particular geographic area and can only make connections to a list of pre-chosen locations. This helps to frustrate the raiders who will try to break into the network from their home (an unapproved source) and roam through the system (unapproved destinations).

Traffic within the TYMNET system travels in TII (T2) format, which only Engines can understand. A thief who managed to intercept data packets could not read T2-format packets.

TYMNET originally introduced variable-sized packets with interleaved customer data to improve flow control, but it also confers security advantages. The TYMNET packets include data from various customers, so no packets move into the system half-filled while other customers wait for access. These packets disguise the data of any individual customer. How easily could potential spies disassemble such a packet to find the specific information they are looking for? Finally, packets don't include the destination's name in any understandable form.

TYMNET tracks suspicious logon patterns. Typically, a person making a concerted attempt to break into a network will program a computer to keep trying to log on with different user names and passwords. What one computer can create, another computer can break. Network computers can recognize a suspicious pattern in these logon attempts. The network will then isolate the telephone number of the would-be thief and take appropriate action.

Illegal Entry to Your System from a Public Packet Network

In addition to security breaches for data travelling in a public packet network, you must also consider the possibility of another subscriber using the network that you share to break into your system. You will understand the seriousness of this potential problem when you realize that your competitors probably use the same PPN that you do (Figure 9-6).

You must also realize that the young people who use breaking into computer systems as an antidote to boredom frequently do so through a PPN. May 1983 saw a well-publicized illegal entry to the GTE-Telenet system. Once past the system's own defenses, the pranksters roamed through several subscriber systems, including a weapons laboratory at Los Alamos, New Mexico. Others can get into your system through the same gateways that you use to connect your system to the PPN. A password system forms the best defense against these raiders.

For a LAN system, where the potential losses to raiders are higher than for a lone host or microcomputer, you might consider disabling the gateway

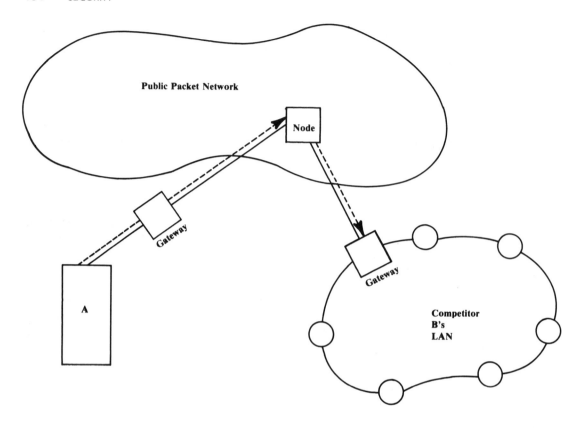

FIGURE 9-6
Customer A uses a VAN to invade customer B's
system.

to the PPN during the evening hours or whenever legitimate users don't need to access the system. Even in this technology-intensive age, don't underestimate the value of pulling the plug.

Choosing Your PPN Security Strategy

At first sight, the greater security of the TYMNET PPN seems to dictate choosing that PPN over other less security-conscious PPNs. You need not so decide. Many customers of GTE-Telenet who prefer more security provide their own security precautions—albeit at their own expense. Other subscribers use TYMNET even though they prefer to do without TYMNET's more secure environment; you can disable many of TYMNET's features on request and some subscribers so request.

Greater security in a PPN carries some costs, regardless of the vendor you choose. A more secure PPN will be more complex to use, requiring more employee training. The additional training time will increase your training costs. The more involved logon procedures will increase the exasperation level of all employees. This may matter more to you than the security of the information you store, send, and receive.

MAKING A SECURITY DECISION

This entire chapter might seem an exercise in paranoia. However, you will not force the dangers to disappear by ignoring them. In fact, the dangers increase with every day because the same factors that make computing and networking so valuable also make espionage so much easier and more profitable. You can choose to ignore the issue of security, or you can choose to take one or more precautions discussed in this chapter. Whatever your ultimate choice, the question deserves a thoughtful decision.

appendix

This appendix contains brief explanations of topics that you may find useful in your data communications and networking work.

1. What is a baud? How do you convert a baud rate to bps?

The baud is a unit of signalling speed, equal to the reciprocal (1/speed) of the speed of the shortest character. Bits per second (bps) equals the number of bits that pass a particular point in a second of time; it is a unit of information transfer. Since a signal pulse is usually equal to a bit, the baud rate and bps usually equal the same number.

With a 2-phase (2-wire) modem, bps equals the baud rate.

With a 4-phase or other modem, you must follow these calculations:

$$\text{bps} = \text{baud rate} \times \text{number of bits per baud}$$

Now, let's start with the number of bits per baud and then substitute in the final equation above.

bits/baud = $\log_2$ (Number of discrete signals levels that can be sent)

With a 4-phase modem, the number of discrete signal levels equals 4.

Example: 1200 baud and 4-phase modem

$$\text{bits/baud} = \log_2 (4)$$
$$\text{bits/baud} = 2$$
$$\text{bps} = 1200 \times 2$$
$$\text{bps} = 2400$$

So with this modem, 1200 baud equals 2400 bps.

---

2.   What is a decibel?

Parents who complain about the decibels of their teenager's rock music imply that the decibel is a measure of loudness, but it isn't.

The decibel (dB) measures the relative strength of the data signal compared to the noise signal.

$$dB = 10 \log_{10} \frac{\text{power level of the data signal}}{\text{power level of the noise signal}}$$

With 23 or more decibels, the error-causing noise will not significantly impact the data signal.

glossary

access method   How the nodes share the path in a LAN.

acknowledgment   A process by which the receiver tells the sender that it received the last data transmission.

address   A logical "location" that allows an operating system and other system/network software to identify specific logical devices.

analog   Representation of data in a continuously graded, rather than in ON/OFF, form; usually uses sound frequencies.

asynchronous (async)   A method of data transmission in which each character has start and stop bits. The sender and receiver need not agree on synchronization before the character arrives.

band   The full range of frequencies available for data transmission.

bandwidth   The size of a band, usually measured in hertz (cycles/second).

baseband   A LAN technology in which data travel to the receiver in the form the sender produces them.

binary   A number system with only two elements, 0 and 1.

bit   The smallest unit of information your computer communicates; a 0 or 1.

block   A group of bytes that travel as a unit. The block includes synchronization, error control, and other information.

bps (bits per second)   The data rate or speed.

broadband   A LAN technology in which data are transferred to the RF range before being transmitted.

burst error   An error that causes a "burst" of flipped bit values in contiguous bits of the data stream.

bus   An architecture in which each device has access to every other object, without a hierarchy of access.

byte   In ASCII systems, 8 bits.

call-back   A security procedure that reduces the danger to public access ports.

character   A letter, number, special printable symbol, or non-printable control symbol.

ciphers   An easily broken form of security for data, usually created with substitution and transposition.

ciphertext   The encrypted message; uses a key to decrypt ciphertext into cleartext.

circuit   A physical connection between sender and receiver.

cleartext   The message that will be encrypted or turned into ciphertext.

code   A collection of symbols with equivalent binary values.

collision   What occurs when two packets try to use the path at the same time.

command frame   An SDLC frame sent by a primary station to a secondary station.

common carrier   Provides basic communication and transportation services to the public.

communications processor   A smart multiplexor; it includes storage and queueing as well as logic functions.

conditioned line   A special low-error transmission line leased from your local telephone company in the U.S.

contention   The competition for access to the path by the LAN's nodes.

control mode   When two stations are exchanging Bisync header information.

controller   A device that controls other devices. The subordinates cannot communicate with the controller or with each other until the controller gives them permission to send.

CPU (Central Processing Unit)   The computer's brain, where logic and control functions occur.

cross-talk   A source of data communication errors; occurs when two data streams interfere with each other electromagnetically.

CSMA   A form of contention in which a station tests the path, then transmits.

cyclical redundancy check   An error-checking character attached to a block of data.

Datagram   A class of Network Layer service best suited to message broadcasting.

Data Link   The second layer of the OSI model, which governs how the bits are logically packaged.

device driver   Deals with the data communications traffic of a device class, providing buffering and other services for a CPU.

digital   The ON/OFF (or 1/0) method of coding data.

digital signature   A very secure protection for data transmission.

digitize   To turn speech into digital data.

false   The 0 logical state; opposite of true.

field   What SDLC frames are divided into.

frame   The unit of data transfer in SDLC.

full-duplex   A connection in which each side can both send and receive simultaneously.

gateway   A logical device that allows LANs to communicate with each other and with other services.

guard bands   Unused frequency ranges, which prevent data bands from interfering with each other.

half-duplex   A connection in which each side can either be sending or receiving, but not both simultaneously.

handshake   The process by which two devices prepare to communicate.

hex (hexadecimal)   The base 16 number system.

high   The "on" state; the logical state equivalent to 1 or true.

high-order bits   Bit positions 4,5,6, or 7; the highest place value bits in a byte.

host computer   A computer that controls or determines the operations of your microcomputer.

hub go-ahead polling   A polling scheme in which a station with nothing to send passes the poll on to the next address in the list.

impulse noise   The major reducible source of data communication errors.

interface   A connection (and usually translator) between two equal and similar objects in a network or other communication system.

interrupt   A signal that a controller uses to stop a subordinate's current task. The subordinate will then wait for the controller to talk.

key   That which acts on cleartext to produce ciphertext.

LAN (local area network)   A network that does its work within a 10-km area.

leased line   A special low-error transmission line, dedicated to your use and leased from your local telephone company in the U.S.

listener   A device that takes data off the GPIB.

listen-only   A device that can only take data off the GPIB.

logical device   A device that can be addressed and accessed. It may or may not be equivalent to a physical device.

low   Opposite of high; a logical state equivalent to 0, or false.

low-order bit   Bit positions 1,2, and 3 in a byte; the lowest place value positions in the byte.

message mode   The mode two Bisync stations are in when they exchange a message.

messages   Complete communication sent as a unit; able to be queued and assigned priorities.

modem   Translates digital data into analog (sound) data, and vice versa.

mux (multiplexor)   A device that allows many slow-speed devices to share a single high-speed data communication line.

NAPLPS (North American Presentation Layer Protocol Syntax) The North American videotex standard.

node   A station in a LAN or other communications system.

octal   The base 8 number system.

packet   Data that travels to its destination without having a complete communication channel between sender and receiver.

PAD (Packet Assembly and Disassembly)   The process of creating packets or disassembling packets into raw data, or a facility that accomplishes this task.

page   The basic unit of videotex service; one screen's worth of information.

parallel   An interface in which all the bits in a byte travel down the wire in parallel.

parity check   A simple error-checking scheme, using the one non-data bit in a byte.

path   The communication medium in a LAN.

pipe   A logical file-system structure that allows files to be shared by computers using different operating systems.

polling   The process by which a controller gives a subordinate permission to transmit.

port (a physical port)   The place where a device connects to the outside world, usually by a cable; it may contain several logical ports.

PPN (Public Packet Network)   A VAN packet-based network; subscribers can transmit packets to any other subscriber of the PPN.

protocol   A procedure for establishing and maintaining communication between two dissimilar objects in a communication system, usually including translation.

response frame   An SDLC frame sent by a subordinate to a primary.

round-robin polling   A polling scheme in which a controller sends the poll to each address in numerical order.

semaphore   Prevents multiple users from writing to (altering) the same file at the same time.

serial   An interface in which the bits in a byte travel down the wire one by one (serially).

server   A LAN device that provides specialized services to other nodes.

signature   The digital model of a word that a voice recognition system uses in its comparisons.

simplex   A connection in which the sender can only send and the receiver can only receive.

socket   The transport address in a LAN.

speaker-dependent   A voice recognition system that can only be used by one person. A speaker-independent system can be used by many people.

standards   Agreements concerning electrical, data transfer, or other computer-related issues.

start bit   Tells the receiver in an asynchronous transmission to start sampling data bits; signals the start of a character of data.

stop bit   Tells the receiver in an asynchronous transmission that the character has ended.

subchannel   The part of the channel that a frequency division multiplexor assigns to each terminal.

subscriber   The user of a teletext or videotex service, a VAN or PPN.

switched line   A communication path that routes data through switching stations.

synchronous   A method of data transmission in which the sender and receiver synchronize to each other before data begin to travel.

synchronization   The process by which a sender and receiver agree on where a character starts and ends.

talker   A device that puts data on the GPIB.

talk-only   A device that can only put data on the GPIB.

teletext   Non-interactive, broadcast text and graphics service.

terminal   The endpoint of a transaction; three types have different capabilities.

token   A bit pattern that tells a LAN station that it now has permission to put a data packet on the path.

transparent mode   A Bisync mode in which you can put control characters into your data stream.

true   The 1 logical state.

VAN (Value-Added Network)   A network providing services greater than those provided by the common carriers.

videotex   An interactive text and graphics service.

Virtual Circuit   A class of Network Layer service that gives 100% error-free transmission and establishes a complete connection between sender and receiver before packet transmission begins.

virtual terminal   A protocol that allows system software to ignore the vast array of different physical terminals the network may have.

voice mail   A message-transmission form in which an actual voice message is digitized, then transmitted.

zero insertion and deletion   Allows you to send five contiguous 1's in an SDLC data stream; the receiver will not confuse these data with the Flag Field.

index